Contemporary Studies in Literature

Eugene Ehrlich, *Columbia University*
Daniel Murphy, *City University of New York*
Series Editors

Volumes include:

Ezra Pound

a collection of criticism edited by Grace Schulman

McGraw-Hill Book Company

New York • St. Louis • San Francisco • London • Düsseldorf
Kuala Lumpur • Mexico • Montreal • Panama • São Paulo
Sydney • Toronto • Johannesburg • New Delhi • Singapore

The editor is grateful to New Directions Publishing Corporation for permission to reprint quotations from Ezra Pound's poetry and prose.

Excerpts of poetry are from: *Personae* by Ezra Pound. Copyright 1926 by Ezra Pound. *The Cantos* of Ezra Pound. Copyright 1934, 1937, 1940, 1948 © 1956, 1959, 1962, 1972 by Ezra Pound. Reprinted by permission of New Directions Publishing Corporation.

Excerpts of prose are from: Ezra Pound, *Guide to Kulchur*. All rights reserved. Copyright © 1970 by Ezra Pound. *Jefferson and / or Mussolini*. Copyright 1935, 1936 by Ezra Pound. *Selected Letters* (1907–1941), D. D. Paige, ed. Copyright 1950 by Ezra Pound. *Pound/Joyce, Letters and Essays*, F. Read, ed. Copyright © 1965, 1966, 1967 by Ezra Pound. *Confucius: The Great Digest and Unwobbling Pivot*. Copyright 1928 by Glenn Hughes. Copyright 1947 by Ezra Pound. Reprinted by permission of New Directions Publishing Corporation.

123456789MUMU7987654

Library of Congress Cataloging in Publication Data

Schulman, Grace, comp.

    Ezra Pound: a collection of criticism

    (Contemporary studies in literature)

    Bibliography: p.
    1. Pound, Ezra Loomis, 1885-1972.
PS3531.082Z834   811'.5'2   74-7254
ISBN 0-07-055634-2

Preface

The present volume is divided into three parts: the first section includes the poet's own testimony and covers the years 1913 to 1962. In "A Retrospect," Ezra Pound names the rules of Imagism and defines his Doctrine of the Image; in "How I Began," the lively account of his arrival in London, he recounts his search for exact visual equivalents of emotions. "Ezra Pound," an interview with Donald Hall, is a portrait of the artist in Rome, making new discoveries about his life and work.

The general essays in the second section discuss aspects of his contribution to twentieth-century literature. In the passages by two of Pound's major contemporaries, T. S. Eliot speaks of his original use of tradition, and Marianne Moore, emphasizing Pound's poetic beliefs and their importance to other artists, suggests their impact on her poetry as well. Sister Bernetta Quinn writes of Ezra Pound in his role as "preceptor," and Hugh Kenner illuminates the poet's use of diction.

In choosing selections for Part Three, which deals with specific works and stages of development, I have concentrated on those passages that assist the beginning reader in exploring the poetry of Ezra Pound. It is my belief that the *Cantos* have unity, and that they incarnate a vision of human wholeness. To know their poetic integrity, however, it is necessary to read them with as much care as Ezra Pound demanded for and gave to other writers. That investigation is rewarding, for he has built his poetry on a clear view of human emotions that endure.

Grace Schulman

Baruch College
City University of New York
June, 1974

Contents

Grace Schulman

Introduction: The Last American

"Somebody said that I am the last American living the tragedy of Europe,"[1] Ezra Pound remarked in Rome in 1962. Although the statement was made in another context, it evokes his lifelong concern with a new American poetry whose sources were found in foreign cultures and in the past.

After a boyhood in Wyncote, Pennsylvania, a college education at the University of Pennsylvania and at Hamilton College, New York, and an aborted career as an instructor at Wabash College, Crawfordsville, Indiana, Pound arrived in London in 1908, carrying his first book of poems, *A Lume Spento*, which had been printed in Venice.[2] Of the five major twentieth-century poets born in America from 1883 to 1888 (William Carlos Williams, 1883; Pound, 1885; Hilda Doolittle, 1886; Marianne Moore, 1887; and T. S. Eliot, 1888), Pound, Eliot, and H. D. had established residence in Europe by the end of the second decade.

Although he remained in Europe for most of his life, Pound retained qualities that are characteristically American. There was in him a rollicking humor that was clearly of our native variety. Too often mistaken for a lack of esteem, Pound's playfulness—jaunty, boisterous, irreverent—was directed at people and things he admired. To T. S. Eliot, he wrote: "It is after all a grrrreat littttttterary period." William Carlos Williams, his college friend, was addressed variously as "Deer Bullll,"

---

[1] *Writers at Work: The* Paris Review *Interviews, Second Series; Edited by George Plimpton; Introduced by Van Wyck Brooks* (New York: Viking, 1963), p. 59.
[2] Early biographical facts, these pages, from *Ezra Pound* by Charles Norman, revised edition (New York: Minerva Press, 1960), pp. 1-35.

1

"Voui, mon vieux coco," "My dear old Hugger-scrunch," and "My Dear Old Sawbukk von Grump." T. E. Lawrence, user of pseudonyms, received a letter from Pound that began: "My Dear Hadji ben Abt el Bakshish, Prince de Mecque, Two-Sworded Samurai, Old Bird, Young Bird, Magister (?) Artium, etc. et quid tibi licet, libet, decet, lubet, etc."[3]

Ezra Pound was generous to his friends. "We have got to do something at once," he wrote to Williams, upon learning that T. S. Eliot was in poor health.[4] The letters in *Pound/Joyce* praise the novelist's work: of *A Portrait of the Artist as a Young Man* the poet wrote, "I think the book is permanent like Flaubert and Stendhal." Also, Pound's letters to Joyce express concern for what he calls Joyce's "pathological eyes." In fact, the American poet made the human but futile attempt to diagnose Joyce's visual disorder, according to a letter of 1916.[5]

When he returned to London in 1911 after a visit in America, Ezra Pound craved the awakening of an American tradition amalgamated with international influences. As Roy Harvey Pearce has pointed out, Pound was to continue the poetry that Walt Whitman had begun in 1855, gradually discovering Whitman's force in himself.[6]

It was only in Europe, though, that Pound recognized he was guided by the spirit of Whitman. Combining his native vigor with his studies of Renaissance literature, Pound wrote, in 1912: "I believe in the immanence of an American Renaissance."[7] In the essay ironically titled *Patria Mia,* Pound said:

> Whitman established the national *timbre.* One may not need him at home. It is in the air, this tonic of his. But if one is abroad; if one is ever likely to forget his birthright, to lose faith, being surrounded by disparagers, one can find, in Whitman, the reassurance. Whitman goes bail for the nation.
>
> (p. 64)

[3] *The Letters of Ezra Pound,* 1907-1941, ed. D. D. Paige (New York: Harcourt, Brace, 1950), pp. 170, 172, 160, 156, 145, 152.

[4] *Letters,* p. 172.

[5] *Pound/Joyce: The Letters of Ezra Pound to James Joyce, with Pound's Essays on Joyce; Edited and with Commentary by Forrest Read* (New York: New Directions, 1957), p. 85.

[6] "Pound, Whitman and the American Epic," in *The Continuity of American Poetry* (Princeton, N. J.: Princeton University Press, 1961), reprinted in Sutton, Walter, ed., *Ezra Pound: A Collection of Critical Essays,* Twentieth Century Views (Englewood Cliffs, N. J.: Prentice-Hall, 1969), pp. 163-167.

[7] *Patria Mia* (Chicago: Ralph Fletcher Seymour, 1950), p. 74.

Sharing Whitman's attraction to science, common lives, and real things, Ezra Pound carried forward the American tradition in its use of what is about, with its implicit insistence on the poet's freedom to contemplate any subject without diminished energy. "They shall find their inspiration in real objects today, symptoms of the past and future," Whitman had prophesied of American poets in the 1855 preface to *Leaves of Grass*,[8] and Ezra Pound was to fulfill that prophecy. But while Whitman created wonder in the landscape and people of his country, Pound extended those national boundaries.

For Ezra Pound, the American awakening was to be an international event, dedicated to a new freedom that would liberate poetry from romantic flaccidity. According to Hugh Kenner, in *The Pound Era*, the poet coined the word *Imagism (Imagisme* as he called it) to describe a quality in the poetry of H. D., a woman he had loved in America and now an admired friend. In the tea room of the British Museum, Pound wrote "H. D. Imagiste" at the bottom of the manuscript of H. D.'s "Hermes of the Ways" before sending it off to Harriet Monroe, founder of *Poetry*, in October 1912.[9] His letter to the pioneer editor comments on how H. D. mingles classic and American elements, for the poet who evokes Hermes uses the "laconic speech of the Imagistes":

> This is the sort of American stuff that I can show here and in Paris without its being ridiculed. Objective—no slither; direct—no excessive use of adjectives, no metaphors that won't permit examination. It's straight talk, straight as the Greek![10]

The merging of American and foreign cultures, of past and present, is implicit in the Imagist movement that generated new energy in modern verse. The rules Pound recalled that he, H. D., and Richard Aldington formulated in 1912 include the direct presentation of the image, the use of no superfluous word, and composition "in the sequence of the musical phrase."[11] Pound called for precise rendering of the natural object, reminiscent of Whitman's belief that the true use of

---

[8] *Walt Whitman's Leaves of Grass: The First (1855) Edition*, ed. Malcolm Cowley (New York: Viking Compass, 1959), p. 22.
[9] Hugh Kenner, *The Pound Era* (Berkeley and Los Angeles, Calif.: University of California Press, 1971), p. 174.
[10] *Letters*, p. 11.
[11] "A Retrospect," *Literary Essays of Ezra Pound*, ed. by T. S. Eliot (Norfolk, Conn.: New Directions, 1954), p. 3. The essay is included in this volume.

the imaginative faculty was "to give ultimate vivification to facts, to science, and to common lives, endowing them with the glows and glories and final illustriousness which belong to every real thing, and to real things only."[12] The new poetry would blend American directness with the finest cadences from the Orient, from medieval and Renaissance Italy, from Greek: *haiku, sestina,* Greek lyric. Pound's maxims, resounding with unwavering certainty ("Go in fear of abstractions"), actually liberated poetry by offering a disciplined alternative to the widespread enslavement to the indefiniteness of post-Symbolist convention.

Ezra Pound's famous Doctrine of the Image is essential to modern poetry, for it articulates his belief in perception as a source of growth:

> An "Image" is that which presents an intellectual and emotional complex in an instant of time. I use the term "complex" rather in the technical sense employed by the new psychologists, such as Hart . . . .
> It is the presentation of such a "complex" instantaneously which gives that sense of sudden liberation; that sense of freedom from time limits and space limits; that sense of sudden growth, which we experience in the presence of the greatest works of art.[13]

For Pound, an image was a dynamic, changing thing, moving as the mind moves and as pictures succeed one another on a cinema screen. Designed to set other associations in motion, images are concrete presentations of objects that also incarnate the act of perception as a continuous process in time. In an essay called "Vorticism," Pound wrote:

> The image is not an idea. It is a radiant node or cluster; it is what I can, and must perforce, call a VORTEX, from which, and through which, and into which, ideas are constantly rushing. . . .[14]

Early and late, Pound's own poetry is built on the tensions between those moments of fiery illumination and his examination of the texture of ordinary existence. In *Personae: The Collected Poems,* "The Alchemist," subtitled "Chant for the Transmutation of Metals," contains an invocation to a goddess to set in motion the transforming power of the

---

[12] "A Backward Glance O'er Travel'd Roads," in *Leaves of Grass: Comprehensive Reader's Edition*, ed. Harold W. Blodgett and Scully Bradley (New York: Norton, 1965), p. 564.

[13] "A Retrospect," p. 4.

[14] *Fortnightly Review*, vol. 96 (1914), p. 470.

imagination that will enable the poet to gaze into the life of things:

> Midonz, gift of the God, gift of the light, gift of
>   the amber of the sun,
>   Give light to the metal.[15]

In the opening lines of "Ballatetta," the poet sees into the radiant world, creating light through music:

> The light became her grace and dwelt among
> Blind eyes and shadows that are formed as men;
> Lo, how the light doth melt us into song . . .

"Francesca" incarnates a clear, sharp image that emerges and dissolves waste, ordering the darkness:

> You came in out of the night
> And there were flowers in your hands,
> Now you will come out of a confusion of people,
> Out of a turmoil of speech about you.
>
> I who have seen you amid the primal things
> Was angry when they spoke your name
> In ordinary places . . .

And in "The River-Merchant's Wife: A Letter," Pound's version of Rihaku's poem on the ordinary theme of a young woman who misses her absent husband, an extraordinary longing is objectified by the presentation of accurate images. Those pictures move as thought moves, each suggesting another that follows. The power of light is manifest in this poem as well, but here the fading of light figures forth the speaker's loss:

> The paired butterflies are already yellow with August
> Over the grass in the West garden;
> They hurt me. I grow older.

Such poems as those, or "Doria," or "Dance Figure," or "Alba," are moving for their passion, for their rightness of cadence, and for a

---

[15]*Personae: The Collected Poems* (New York: Horace Liveright, 1926; New Directions, 1969). Verse quotations, with the exception of the *Cantos*, are from the New Directions edition.

tough-minded insistence on giving exact visual equations of emotions. Because that principle of equation is basic to magical incantations and to scientific formulae, the effect is simultaneously mysterious and accurate.

It is meaningful to consider how these themes and effects endured in his later work, for the passion in Ezra Pound's art is to be found in the whole of his poetry, not only in one individual part.

From the beginning of his career, the poet used disguises as projections of a changing self: "Masks" is the title of a poem in *A Lume Spento*, and the collected edition is called *Personae*. Through the mask the contemporary poet is clearly audible, for he speaks as troubadour or as alchemist in order to gain a lucid perspective on current circumstance. The poet fuses ancient and modern sensibilities for a vision of the present that is astonishing for the darkness that his insight renders intelligible. Using roles, he captures moments of light: "Remember this fire" is that chant of "The Alchemist," and the speaker of "Dance Figure" utters, "Thy face is a river with lights." The splendid moment is sadly transient, however, as we find in "Praise of Ysolt":

> My song was ablaze with her and she went from me
> As flame leaveth the embers so went she unto new forests . . .

And in "De Aegypto," the poet chants in his role as another of the singers:

> I am flame that riseth in the sun,
> I, even I, who fly with the swallows.

In the early poems, moments of intense awareness are times of perceptual change. "The Tree" begins:

> I stood still and was a tree amid the wood
> Knowing the truth of things unseen before . . .

Just as the speaker of "A Tree" perceives clarity "unseen before" by means of his own metamorphosis, the poet in various guises explores a shifting reality. Although the theme of metamorphosis is basic to Pound's poetry, we learn in Canto V of its importance in the poetic process:

> Air, fire, the pale soft light.
> Topaz I manage, and three sorts of blue;

> but on the barb of time.
> The fire? always, and the vision always,
> Ear dull, perhaps, with the vision, flitting
> And fading at will. . . .[16]

Metamorphosis, we learn, is the function of the artist, who manages the light by perceiving the changing relationship of things. And this vision of the truth of things is built on his belief in the image as a dynamic picture, in continuous motion, containing within itself the thoughts and feelings of the viewer.

Perceptual change is a theme that is essential to the *Cantos*, for in that poem the quest for a beauty that endures involves a penetrating vision of the transformation of things. Hugh Kenner, in *The Poetry of Ezra Pound*, helpfully located the central experience of the *Cantos* as the "periplum, the voyage of discovery among facts."[17] And, adding to this insight, M. L. Rosenthal pointed out that the protagonist of the *Cantos* is a composite figure. Of the periplum he wrote: "In the first two cantos . . . the 'periplum' of the sequence emerges into view. Three main value-referents are established: a sexually and aesthetically creative world-view, in which artistic and mythical tradition provides the main axes; the worship of Bacchus-Dionysus-Zagreus as the best symbol of creativity in action; and the multiple hero—poet, voyager, prophet, observer, thinker."[18]

The *Cantos*, which were begun in 1904[19] and represent the work of a lifetime, have a unity that is based on a process of making intelligible the disparate facts of present truth. The periplum is the incarnation of the vision of a changing reality. "I have seen" is a recurrent phrase in Pound's early lyrics, recalling Walt Whitman's "I perceive," a frequent exclamation in *Leaves of Grass*. "I have seen what I have seen" is the outcry that signals the emergence of the periplum in the *Cantos*. To discover a shining god in the present is the purpose of navigating through the past and into other worlds, just as the poet found a new

[16] *The* Cantos *of Ezra Pound; 1948; Revised Edition (Cantos 1-117), Incorporating* Thrones and Drafts & Fragments (New York: New Directions, 1970), p. 21. All quotations from the *Cantos* are in this edition.

[17] Hugh Kenner, *The Poetry of Ezra Pound* (Norfolk, Conn.: New Directions, 1951), p. 103.

[18] M. L. Rosenthal, *A Primer of Ezra Pound* (New York: Macmillan, 1960), pp. 45-46.

[19] Pound says this in "Ezra Pound," *Writers at Work: The* Paris Review *Interviews: Second Series, Edited by George Plimpton; Introduced by Van Wyck Brooks* (New York, 1963), p. 38.

American poetry by searching beyond the country's boundaries. If Ezra Pound was one of the first writers to internationalize his native poetry, he was one of the last writers for whom it would ever be possible to remain purely national. For after his example, the consciousness that contained past and present, Europe and America, became charted territory for poets of the world.

Part I

The Poet's Views

Ezra Pound

A Retrospect [1]

There has been so much scribbling about a new fashion in poetry, that I may perhaps be pardoned this brief recapitulation and retrospect.

In the spring or early summer of 1912, "H. D.," Richard Aldington and myself decided that we were agreed upon the three principles following:

1. Direct treatment of the "thing" whether subjective or objective.
2. To use absolutely no word that does not contribute to the presentation.
3. As regarding rhythm: to compose in the sequence of the musical phrase, not in sequence of a metronome.

Upon many points of taste and of predilection we differed, but agreeing upon these three positions we thought we had as much right to a group name, at least as much right, as a number of French "schools" proclaimed by Mr. Flint in the August number of Harold Monro's magazine for 1911.

This school has since been "joined" or "followed" by numerous people who, whatever their merits, do not show any signs of agreeing

[1] A group of early essays and notes which appeared under this title in *Pavannes and Divisions* (1918). "A Few Don'ts" was first printed in *Poetry*, I, 6 (March, 1913).

From The Literary Essays of Ezra Pound: *Edited with an Introduction by T. S. Eliot (Norfolk, Conn.: New Directions, 1954). Copyright 1918 by Ezra Pound. Reprinted by permission of New Directions Publishing Corporation and Faber and Faber Ltd.*

with the second specification. Indeed *vers libre* has become as prolix
and as verbose as any of the flaccid varieties that preceded it. It has
brought faults of its own. The actual language and phrasing is often as
bad as that of our elders without even the excuse that the words are
shovelled in to fill a metric pattern or to complete the noise of a rhyme-
sound. Whether or no the phrases followed by the followers are musical
must be left to the reader's decision. At times I can find a marked
meter in *"vers libre,"* as stale and hackneyed as any pseudo-Swin-
burnian, at times the writers seem to follow no musical structure whatever. But it is, on the whole, good that the field should be ploughed.
Perhaps a few good poems have come from the new method, and if so
it is justified.

Criticism is not a circumscription or a set of prohibitions. It provides fixed points of departure. It may startle a dull reader into alert-
ness. That little of it which is good is mostly in stray phrases; or if it be
an older artist helping a younger it is in great measure but rules of
thumb, cautions gained by experience.

I set together a few phrases on practical working about the time the
first remarks on imagisme were published. The first use of the word
"Imagiste" was in my note to T. E. Hulme's five poems, printed at the
end of my "Ripostes" in the autumn of 1912. I reprint my cautions
from *Poetry* for March, 1913.

A FEW DON'TS

An "Image" is that which presents an intellectual and emotional
complex in an instant of time. I use the term "complex" rather in the
technical sense employed by the newer psychologists, such as Hart,
though we might not agree absolutely in our application.

It is the presentation of such a "complex" instantaneously which
gives that sense of sudden liberation; that sense of freedom from time
limits and space limits; that sense of sudden growth, which we experience in the presence of the greatest works of art.

It is better to present one Image in a lifetime than to produce
voluminous works.

All this, however, some may consider open to debate. The immediate necessity is to tabulate A List of Don'ts for those beginning to
write verses. I can not pull all of them into Mosaic negative.

To begin with, consider the three propositions (demanding direct
treatment, economy of words, and the sequence of the musical phrase),
not as dogma—never consider anything as dogma—but as the result of
long contemplation, which, even if it is some one else's contemplation,
may be worth consideration.

Pay no attention to the criticism of men who have never themselves written a notable work. Consider the discrepancies between the actual writing of the Greek poets and dramatists, and the theories of the Graeco-Roman grammarians, concocted to explain their metres.

LANGUAGE

Use no superfluous word, no adjective which does not reveal something.

Don't use such an expression as "dim lands *of peace.*" It dulls the image. It mixes an abstraction with the concrete. It comes from the writer's not realizing that the natural object is always the *adequate* symbol.

Go in fear of abstractions. Do not retell in mediocre verse what has already been done in good prose. Don't think any intelligent person is going to be deceived when you try to shirk all the difficulties of the unspeakably difficult art of good prose by chopping your compositon into line lengths.

What the expert is tired of today the public will be tired of tomorrow.

Don't imagine that the art of poetry is any simpler than the art of music, or that you can please the expert before you have spent at least as much effort on the art of verse as the average piano teacher spends on the art of music.

Be influenced by as many great artists as you can, but have the decency either to acknowledge the debt outright, or to try to conceal it.

Don't allow "influence" to mean merely that you mop up the particular decorative vocabulary of some one or two poets whom you happen to admire. A Turkish war correspondent was recently caught red-handed babbling in his despatches of "dove-grey" hills, or else it was "pearl-pale," I can not remember.

Use either no ornament or good ornament.

RHYTHM AND RHYME

Let the candidate fill his mind with the finest cadences he can discover, preferably in a foreign language,[2] so that the meaning of the

---

[2] This is for rhythm, his vocabulary must of course be found in his native tongue.

words may be less likely to divert his attention from the movement; e.g. Saxon charms, Hebridean Folk Songs, the verse of Dante, and the lyrics of Shakespeare—if he can dissociate the vocabulary from the cadence. Let him dissect the lyrics of Goethe coldly into their component sound values, syllables long and short, stressed and unstressed, into vowels and consonants.

It is not necessary that a poem should rely on its music, but if it does rely on its music that music must be such as will delight the expert.

Let the neophyte know assonance and alliteration, rhyme immediate and delayed, simple and polyphonic, as a musician would expect to know harmony and counterpoint and all the minutiae of his craft. No time is too great to give to these matters or to any one of them, even if the artist seldom have need of them.

Don't imagine that a thing will "go" in verse just because it's too dull to go in prose.

Don't be "viewy"—leave that to the writers of pretty little philosophic essays. Don't be descriptive; remember that the painter can describe a landscape much better than you can, and that he has to know a deal more about it.

When Shakespeare talks of the "Dawn in russet mantle clad" he presents something which the painter does not present. There is in this line of his nothing that one can call description; he presents.

Consider the way of the scientists rather than the way of an advertising agent for a new soap.

The scientist does not expect to be acclaimed as a great scientist until he has *discovered* something. He begins by learning what has been discovered already. He goes from that point onward. He does not bank on being a charming fellow personally. He does not expect his friends to applaud the results of his freshman class work. Freshmen in poetry are unfortunately not confined to a definite and recognizable class room. They are "all over the shop." Is it any wonder "the public is indifferent to poetry"?

Don't chop your stuff into separate *iambs*. Don't make each line stop dead at the end, and then begin every next line with a heave. Let the beginning of the next line catch the rise of the rhythm wave, unless you want a definite longish pause.

In short, behave as a musician, a good musician, when dealing with that phase of your art which has exact parallels in music. The same laws govern, and you are bound by no others.

Naturally, your rhythmic structure should not destroy the shape of your words, or their natural sound, or their meaning. It is improbable that, at the start, you will be able to get a rhythm-structure strong enough to affect them very much, though you may fall a victim to all sorts of false stopping due to line ends and cæsurae.

The Musician can rely on pitch and the volume of the orchestra. You cannot. The term harmony is misapplied in poetry; it refers to simultaneous sounds of different pitch. There is, however, in the best verse a sort of residue of sound which remains in the ear of the hearer and acts more or less as an organ-base.

A rhyme must have in it some slight element of surprise if it is to give pleasure; it need not be bizarre or curious, but it must be well used if used at all.

Vide further Vildrac and Duhamel's notes on rhyme in *"Technique Poétique."*

That part of your poetry which strikes upon the imaginative *eye* of the reader will lose nothing by translation into a foreign tongue; that which appeals to the ear can reach only those who take it in the original.

Consider the definiteness of Dante's presentation, as compared with Milton's rhetoric. Read as much of Wordsworth as does not seem too unutterably dull.[3]

If you want the gist of the matter go to Sappho, Catullus, Villon, Heine when he is in the vein, Gautier when he is not too frigid; or, if you have not the tongues, seek out the leisurely Chaucer. Good prose will do you no harm, and there is good discipline to be had by trying to write it.

Translation is likewise good training, if you find that your original matter "wobbles" when you try to rewrite it. The meaning of the poem to be translated can not "wobble."

If you are using a symmetrical form, don't put in what you want to say and then fill up the remaining vacuums with slush.

Don't mess up the perception of one sense by trying to define it in terms of another. This is usually only the result of being too lazy to find the exact word. To this clause there are possibly exceptions.

The first three simple prescriptions will throw out nine-tenths of all the bad poetry now accepted as standard and classic; and will prevent you from many a crime of production.

". . . Mais d'abord il faut être un poète," as MM. Duhamel and Vildrac have said at the end of their little book, *"Notes sur la Technique Poétique."*

Since March 1913, Ford Madox Hueffer has pointed out that

---

[3] *Vide infra.*

Wordsworth was so intent on the ordinary or plain word that he never thought of hunting for *le mot juste.*

John Butler Yeats has handled or man-handled Wordsworth and the Victorians, and his criticism, contained in letters to his son, is now printed and available.

I do not like writing *about* art, my first, at least I think it was my first essay on the subject, was a protest against it.

PROLEGOMENA[4]

Time was when the poet lay in a green field with his head against a tree and played his diversion on a ha'penny whistle, and Caesar's predecessors conquered the earth, and the predecessors of golden Crassus embezzled, and fashions had their say, and let him alone. And presumably he was fairly content in this circumstance, for I have small doubt that the occasional passerby, being attracted by curiosity to know why any one should lie under a tree and blow diversion on a ha'penny whistle, came and conversed with him, and that among these passers-by there was on occasion a person of charm or a young lady who had not read *Man and Superman;* and looking back upon this naive state of affairs we call it the age of gold.

Metastasio, and he should know if any one, assures us that this age endures—even though the modern poet is expected to holloa his verses down a speaking tube to the editors of cheap magazines—S. S. McClure, or some one of that sort—even though hordes of authors meet in dreariness and drink healths to the "Copyright Bill"; even though these things be, the age of gold pertains. Imperceivably, if you like, but pertains. You meet unkempt Amyclas in a Soho restaurant and chant together of dead and forgotten things—it is a manner of speech among poets to chant of dead, half-forgotten things, there seems no special harm in it; it has always been done—and it's rather better to be a clerk in the Post Office than to look after a lot of stinking, verminous sheep—and at another hour of the day one substitutes the drawing-room for the restaurant and tea is probably more palatable than mead and mare's milk, and little cakes than honey. And in this fashion one survives the resignation of Mr. Balfour, and the iniquities of the American customs-house, *e quel bufera infernal,* the periodical press. And then in the middle of it, there being apparently no other person at

[4]*Poetry and Drama* (then the *Poetry Review,* edited by Harold Monro), Feb. 1912.

once capable and available one is stopped and asked to explain oneself.

I begin on the chord thus querulous, for I would much rather lie on what is left of Catullus' parlour floor and speculate the azure beneath it and the hills off to Salo and Riva with their forgotten gods moving unhindered amongst them, than discuss any processes and theories of art whatsoever. I would rather play tennis. I shall not argue.

CREDO

Rhythm. – I believe in an "absolute rhythm," a rhythm, that is, in poetry which corresponds exactly to the emotion or shade of emotion to be expressed. A man's rhythm must be interpretative, it will be. therefore, in the end, his own, uncounterfeiting, uncounterfeitable.

Symbols. – I believe that the proper and perfect symbol is the natural object, that if a man use "symbols" he must so use them that their symbolic function does not obtrude; so that *a* sense, and the poetic quality of the passage, is not lost to those who do not understand the symbol as such, to whom, for instance, a hawk is a hawk.

Technique. – I believe in technique as the test of a man's sincerity; in law when it is ascertainable; in the trampling down of every convention that impedes or obscures the determination of the law, or the precise rendering of the impulse.

Form. – I think there is a "fluid" as well as a "solid" content, that some poems may have form as a tree has form, some as water poured into a vase. That most symmetrical forms have certain uses. That a vast number of subjects cannot be precisely, and therefore not properly rendered in symmetrical forms.

"Thinking that alone worthy wherein the whole art is employed."[5] I think the artist should master all known forms and systems of metric, and I have with some persistence set about doing this, searching particularly into those periods wherein the systems came to birth or attained their maturity. It has been complained, with some justice, that I dump my note-books on the public. I think that only after a long struggle will poetry attain such a degree of development, or, if you will, modernity, that it will vitally concern people who are accustomed, in prose, to Henry James and Anatole France, in music to Debussy. I am constantly contending that it took two centuries of Provence and one of Tuscany to develop the media of Dante's masterwork, that it

[5] Dante, *De Volgari Eloquio.*

took the latinists of the Renaissance, and the Pleiade, and his own age of painted speech to prepare Shakespeare his tools. It is tremendously important that great poetry be written, it makes no jot of difference who writes it. The experimental demonstrations of one man may save the time of many—hence my furore over Arnaut Daniel—if a man's experiments try out one new rime, or dispense conclusively with one iota of currently accepted nonsense, he is merely playing fair with his colleagues when he chalks up his result.

No man ever writes very much poetry that "matters." In bulk, that is, no one produces much that is final, and when a man is not doing this highest thing, this saying the thing once for all and perfectly; when he is not matching Ποικιλόθρον', ἀθάνατ' 'Αφρόδιτα, or "Hist—said Kate the Queen," he had much better be making the sorts of experiment which may be of use to him in his later work, or to his successors.

"The lyf so short, the craft so long to lerne." It is a foolish thing for a man to begin his work on a too narrow foundation, it is a disgraceful thing for a man's work not to show steady growth and increasing fineness from first to last.

As for "adaptations"; one finds that all the old masters of painting recommend to their pupils that they begin by copying masterwork, and proceed to their own composition.

As for "Every man his own poet," the more every man knows about poetry the better. I believe in every one writing poetry who wants to; most do. I believe in every man knowing enough of music to play "God bless our home" on the harmonium, but I do not believe in every man giving concerts and printing his sin.

The mastery of any art is the work of a lifetime. I should not discriminate between the "amateur" and the "professional." Or rather I should discriminate quite often in favour of the amateur, but I should discriminate between the amateur and the expert. It is certain that the present chaos will endure until the Art of poetry has been preached down the amateur gullet, until there is such a general understanding of the fact that poetry is an art and not a pastime; such a knowledge of technique; of technique of surface and technique of content, that the amateurs will cease to try to drown out the masters.

If a certain thing was said once for all in Atlantis or Arcadia, in 450 Before Christ or in 1290 after, it is not for us moderns to go saying it over, or to go obscuring the memory of the dead by saying the same thing with less skill and less conviction.

My pawing over the ancients and semi-ancients has been one struggle to find out what has been done, once for all, better than it can ever be done again, and to find out what remains for us to do, and plenty does remain, for if we feel the same emotions as those which launched the thousand ships, it is quite certain that we come on these feelings differently, through different nuances, by different intellectual gradations. Each age has its own abounding gifts yet only some ages transmute them into matter of duration. No good poetry is ever written in a manner twenty years old, for to write in such a manner shows conclusively that the writer thinks from books, convention and *cliché*, and not from life, yet a man feeling the divorce of life and his art may naturally try to resurrect a forgotten mode if he finds in that mode some leaven, or if he think he sees in it some element lacking in contemporary art which might unite that art again to its sustenance, life.

In the art of Daniel and Cavalcanti, I have seen that precision which I miss in the Victorians, that explicit rendering, be it of external nature, or of emotion. Their testimony is of the eyewitness, their symptoms are first hand.

As for the nineteenth century, with all respect to its achievements, I think we shall look back upon it as a rather blurry, messy sort of a period, a rather sentimentalistic, mannerish sort of a period. I say this without any self-righteousness, with no self-satisfaction.

As for there being a "movement" or my being of it; the conception of poetry as a "pure act" in the sense in which I use the term, revived with Swinburne. From the puritanical revolt to Swinburne, poetry had been merely the vehicle—yes, definitely, Arthur Symon's scruples and feelings about the word not withholding—the ox-cart and post-chaise for transmitting thoughts poetic or otherwise. And perhaps the "great Victorians," though it is doubtful, and assuredly the "nineties" continued the development of the art, confining their improvements, however, chiefly to sound and to refinements of manner.

Mr. Yeats has once and for all stripped English poetry of its perdamnable rhetoric. He has boiled away all that is not poetic—and a good deal that is. He has become a classic in his own lifetime and *nel mezzo del cammin.* He has made our poetic idiom a thing pliable, a speech without inversions.

Robert Bridges, Maurice Hewlett and Frederic Manning are[6] in their different ways seriously concerned with overhauling the metric, in testing the language and its adaptability to certain modes. Ford Hueffer is making some sort of experiments in modernity. The Provost of Oriel continues his translation of the *Divina Commedia.*

As to Twentieth century poetry, and the poetry which I expect to

[6](Dec. 1911).

see written during the next decade or so, it will, I think, move against
poppy-cock, it will be harder and saner, it will be what Mr. Hewlett
calls "nearer the bone." It will be as much like granite as it can be,
its force will lie in its truth, its interpretative power (of course, poetic
force does always rest there); I mean it will not try to seem forcible by
rhetorical din, and luxurious riot. We will have fewer painted adjectives
impeding the shock and stroke of it. At least for myself, I want it so,
austere, direct, free from emotional slither.

What is there now, in 1917, to be added?

RE VERS LIBRE

I think the desire for vers libre is due to the sense of quantity
reasserting itself after years of starvation. But I doubt if we can take
over, for English, the rules of quantity laid down for Greek and Latin,
mostly by Latin grammarinas.

I think one should write vers libre only when one "must," that is
to say, only when the "thing" builds up a rhythm more beautiful than
that of set metres, or more real, more a part of the emotion of the
"thing," more germane, intimate, interpretative than the measure of
regular accentual verse; a rhythm which discontents one with set
iambic or set anapaestic.

Eliot has said the thing very well when he said, "No *vers* is *libre* for
the man who wants to do a good job."

As a matter of detail, there is vers libre with accent heavily marked
as a drum-beat (as par example my "Dance Figure"), and on the other
hand I think I have gone as far as can profitably be gone in the other
direction (and perhaps too far). I mean I do not think one can use to
any advantage rhythms much more tenuous and imperceptible than
some I have used. I think progress lies rather in an attempt to ap-
proximate classical quantitative metres (NOT to copy them) than in a
carelessness regarding such things.[7]

I agree with John Yeats on the relation of beauty to certitude. I
prefer satire, which is due to emotion, to any sham of emotion.

I have had to write, or at least I have written a good deal about
art, sculpture, painting and poetry. I have seen what seemed to me
the best of contemporary work reviled and obstructed. Can any one
write prose of permanent or durable interest when he is merely saying
for one year what nearly every one will say at the end of three or four

[7]Let me date this statement 20 Aug. 1917.

years? I have been battistrada for a sculptor, a painter, a novelist, several poets. I wrote also of certain French writers in *The New Age* in nineteen twelve or eleven.

I would much rather that people would look at Brzeska's sculpture and Lewis's drawings, and that they would read Joyce, Jules Romains, Eliot, than that they should read what I have said of these men, or that I should be asked to republish argumentative essays and reviews.

All that the critic can do for the reader or audience or spectator is to focus his gaze or audition. Rightly or wrongly I think my blasts and essays have done their work, and that more people are now likely to go to the sources than are likely to read this book.

Jammes's "Existences" in *"La Triomphe de la Vie"* is available. So are his early poems. I think we need a convenient anthology rather than descriptive criticism. Carl Sandburg wrote me from Chicago, "It's hell when poets can't afford to buy each other's books." Half the people who care, only borrow. In America so few people know each other that the difficulty lies more than half in distribution. Perhaps one should make an anthology: Romains's "Un Etre en Marche" and "Prières," Vildrac's "Visite." Retrospectively the fine wrought work of Laforgue, the flashes of Rimbaud, the hard-bit lines of Tristan Corbière, Tailhade's sketches in "Poèmes Aristophanesques," the "Litanies" of de Gourmont.

It is difficult at all times to write of the fine arts, it is almost impossible unless one can accompany one's prose with many reproductions. Still I would seize this chance or any chance to reaffirm my belief in Wyndham Lewis's genius, both in his drawings and his writings. And I would name an out of the way prose book, the *"Scenes and Portraits"* of Frederic Manning, as well as James Joyce's short stories and novel, "Dubliners" and the now well known "Portrait of the Artist" as well as Lewis' "Tarr," if, that is, I may treat my strange reader as if he were a new friend come into the room, intent on ransacking my bookshelf.

ONLY EMOTION ENDURES

"Only emotion endures." Surely it is better for me to name over the few beautiful poems that still ring in my head than for me to search my flat for back numbers of periodicals and rearrange all that I have said about friendly and hostile writers.

The first twelve lines of Padraic Colum's "Drover"; his "O Woman shapely as a swan, on your account I shall not die"; Joyce's "I hear an army"; the lines of Yeats that ring in my head and in the heads of all young men of my time who care for poetry; Braseal and the Fisherman, "The fire that stirs about her when she stirs"; the later lines of "The Scholars," the faces of the Magi; William Carlos Williams's "Postlude," Aldington's version of "Atthis," and "H. D.'s" waves like pine tops, and her verse in "Des Imagistes" the first anthology; Hueffer's "How red your lips are" in his translation from Von der Vogelweide, his "Three Ten," the general effect of his "On Heaven"; his sense of the prose values or prose qualities in poetry; his ability to write poems that half-chant and are spoiled by a musician's additions; beyond these a poem by Alice Corbin, "One City Only," and another ending "But sliding water over a stone." These things have worn smooth in my head and I am not through with them, nor with Aldington's "In Via Sestina" nor his other poems in "Des Imagistes," though people have told me their flaws. It may be that their content is too much embedded in me for me to look back at the words.

I am almost a different person when I come to take up the argument for Eliot's poems.

Ezra Pound

How I Began

If the verb is put in the past tense there is very little to be said about this matter.

The artist is always beginning. Any work of art which is not a beginning, an invention, a discovery, is of little worth. The very name Troubadour means a "finder," one who discovers.

So far as the public is concerned my "career" has been of the simplest; during the first five years of it I had exactly one brief poem accepted by one American magazine, although I had during that time submitted "La Fraisne" and various other poems now held as a part of my best work. Net result of my activities in case, five dollars which works out to about 4s. 3d. per year.

Mr. Elkin Mathews was the first publisher to whom I submitted my work in London. He printed my first three volumes, "Personae," "Exultations," and "Canzoni," at his own expense. So far as I can remember our only discussion of business was as follows:—

Mr. E. M.: "Ah, eh, do you care to contribute to the costs of publishing?"

Mr. E. P.: "I've got a shilling in my clothes, if that's any use to you."

Mr. E. M.: "Oh well, I rather want to publish 'em anyhow."

From T. P.'s Weekly, *June 6, 1913. All rights reserved. Reprinted by permission of New Directions Publishing Corporation, Agents for the Estate of Ezra Pound. Also appears in* Stony Brook, *1/2 (Post-Fall, 1968).*

I have not yet received a brass farthing from these books, nor do I think that Mr. Mathews has up to date a clear balance against his expenses. One's name is known, in so far as it is known at all widely, through hearsay and reviews and through a wholesale quotation.

My books have made me friends. I came to London with £3 knowing no one.

I had been hungry all my life for "interesting people." I wanted to meet certain men whose work I admired. I have done this. I have had good talk in plenty.

I have paid a certain price. I have endured a certain amount of inconvenience, enough to put an edge on my enjoyment. I believe I have had more solid pleasure in life than any fellow of my years whom I have ever met.

I have "known many men's manners and seen many cities."

Besides knowing living artists I have come in touch with the tradition of the dead. I have had in this the same sort of pleasure that a schoolboy has in hearing of the star plays of former athletes. I have renewed my boyhood. I have repeated the sort of thrill that I used to have in hearing of the deeds of T. Truxton Hare: the sort that future Freshmen will have in hearing how "Mike" Bennet stopped Weeks. I have relished this or that about "old Browning," or Shelley sliding down his front banister "with almost incredible rapidity."

There is more, however, in this sort of Apostolic Succession than a ludicrous anecdote, for people whose minds have been enriched by contact with men of genius retain the effects of it.

I have enjoyed meeting Victorians and Pre-Raphaelites and men of the nineties through their friends. I have seen Keats' proof sheets, I have had personal tradition of his time at second-hand. This, perhaps, means little to a Londoner, but it is good fun if you have grown up regarding such things as about as distant as Ghengis Khan or the days of Lope de Vega.

If by the question "How I began?" you mean "How did I learn my trade?" it is much too long to answer, and the details would be too technical.

I knew at fifteen pretty much what I wanted to do. I believed that the "Impulse" is with the gods; that technique is a man's own responsibility. A man either is or is not a great poet, that is not within his control, it is the lightning from heaven, the "fire of the gods," or whatever you choose to call it.

His recording instrument is in his own charge. It is his own fault if he does not become a good artist—even a flawless artist.

I resolved that at thirty I would know more about poetry than any man living, that I would know the dynamic content from the shell, that

I would know what was accounted poetry everywhere, what part of poetry was "indestructible," what part could *not be lost* by translation, and—scarcely less important—what effects were obtainable in *one* language only and were utterly incapable of being translated.

In this search I learned more or less of nine languages, I read Oriental stuff in translations, I fought every University regulation and every professor who tried to make me learn anything except this, or who bothered me with "requirements for degrees."

Of course, no amount of scholarship will help a man to write poetry, it may even be regarded as a great burden and hindrance, but it does help him to destroy a certain percentage of his failures. It keeps him discontented with mediocrity.

I have written a deal about technique for I detest a botch in a poem or in a donkey engine. I detest people who are content with botches. I detest a satisfaction with second-rateness.

As touching the Impulse, that is another affair. You may even call it "Inspiration." I do not mind the term, although it is in great disfavour with those who never experience the light of it.

The Impulse is a very different thing from the *furor scribendi*, which is a sort of emotional excitement due, I think, to weakness, and often preceding or accompanying early work. It means that the subject has you, not you the subject. There is no formula for the Impulse. Each poem must be a new and strange adventure if it is worth recording at all.

I know that for days the "Night Litany" seemed a thing so little my own that I could not bring myself to sign it. In the case of the "Goodly Fare" I was not excited until some hours after I had written it. I had been the evening before in the "Turkish Coffee" café in Soho. I had been made very angry by a certain sort of cheap irreverence which was new to me. I had lain awake most of the night. I got up rather late in the morning and started for the Museum with the first four lines in my head. I wrote the rest of poem at a sitting, on the left side of the reading-room, with scarcely any erasures. I lunched at the Vienna Café, and later in the afternoon, being unable to study, I peddled the poem about Fleet Street, for I began to realize that for the first time in my life I had written something that "everyone could understand," and I wanted it to go to the people.

The poem was not accepted. I think the "Evening Standard" was the only office where it was even considered. Mr. Ford Madox Hueffer first printed the poem in his review some three months afterwards.

My other "vigorous" poem, the "Alta forte" [*sic*] was also written in the British Museum reading-room. I had had Do Bom on my mind. I had found him untranslatable. Then it occurred to me that I might present him in this manner. I wanted the curious involution and recurrence of the Sestina. I knew more or less of the arrangement. I wrote the first strophe and then went to the Museum to make sure of the right order of permutations, for I was then living in Langham Street, next to the "pub," and had hardly any books with me. I did the rest of the poem at a sitting. Technically it is one of my best, though a poem on such a theme could never be very important.

I waited three years to find the words for "Picadilly," it is eight lines long, and they tell me now it is "sentiment." For well over a year I have been trying to make a poem of a very beautiful thing that befell me in the Paris Underground. I got out of a train at, I think, La Concorde and in the jostle I saw a beautiful face, and then, turning suddenly, another and another, and then a beautiful child's face, and then another beautiful face. All that day I tried to find words for what this made me feel. That night as I went home along the rue Raynouard I was still trying. I could get nothing but spots of colour. I remember thinking that if I had been a painter I might have started a wholly new school of painting. I tried to write the poem weeks afterwards in Italy but found it useless. Then only the other night, wondering how I should tell the adventure, it struck me that in Japan, where a work of art is not estimated by its acreage and where sixteen syllables are counted enough for a poem if you arrange and punctuate them properly, one might make a very little poem which would be translated about as follows:

> "The apparition of these faces in the crowd:
> "Petals on a wet, black bough."

And there, or in some other very old, very quiet civilisation, some one else might understand the significance.

Donald Hall

"Ezra Pound," an Interview

•   •   •

Interviewer: You are nearly through the *Cantos* now, and this sets me to wondering about their beginning. In 1916 you wrote a letter in which you talked about trying to write a version of Andreas Divus in Seafarer rhythms. This sounds like a reference to Canto 1. Did you begin the *Cantos* in 1916?

Pound: I began the *Cantos* about 1904, I suppose. I had various schemes, starting in 1904 or 1905. The problem was to get a form—something elastic enough to take the necessary material. It had to be a form that wouldn't exclude something merely because it didn't fit. In the first sketches, a draft of the present first *Canto* was the third.

Obviously you haven't got a nice little road map such as the middle ages possessed of Heaven. Only a musical form would take the material, and the Confucian universe as I see it is a universe of interacting strains and tensions.

Interviewer: Had your interest in Confucius begun in 1904?

Pound: No, the first thing was this: you had six centuries that hadn't been packaged. It was a question of dealing with material that wasn't in the *Divina Commedia*. Hugo did a *Légende des Siècles* that wasn't an evaluative affair but just bits of history strung together. The problem was to build up a circle of reference taking the modern mind to be the mediaeval mind with wash after wash of classical culture poured over it since the Renaissance. That was the psyche, if you like. One had to deal with one's own subject.

Interviewer: It must be thirty or thirty-five years since you have written any poetry outside the *Cantos*, except for the Alfred Venison poems. Why is this?

Pound: I got to the point where, apart from an occasional lighter impulse, what I had to say fitted the general scheme. There has been a good deal of work thrown away because one is attracted to an historic character and then finds that he doesn't function within my form, doesn't embody a value needed. I have tried to make the *Cantos* historic (Vid. G. Giovannini, *re* relation history to tragedy. Two articles ten years apart in some philological periodical, not source material but relevant) but not fiction. The material one wants to fit in doesn't always work. If the stone isn't hard enough to maintain the form, it has to go out.

Interviewer: When you write a *Canto* now, how do you plan it? Do you follow a special course of reading for each one?

Pound: One isn't necessarily reading. One is working on the life vouchsafed, I should think. I don't know about method. The *what* is so much more important than how.

Interviewer: Yet when you were a young man, your interest in poetry concentrated on form. Your professionalism, and your devotion to technique, became proverbial. In the last thirty years, you have traded your interest in form for an interest in content. Was the change on principle?

Pound: I think I've covered that. Technique is the test of sincerity. If a thing isn't worth getting the technique to say, it is of inferior value. All that must be regarded as exercise. Richter in his *Treatise on Harmony*, you see, says, "These are the principles of harmony and counterpoint; they have nothing whatever to do with composition, which is quite a separate activity." The statement, which somebody made, that you couldn't write Provençal canzoni forms in English, is false. The question of whether it was advisable or not was another matter. When there wasn't the criterion of natural language without inversion, those forms were natural, and they realized them with music. In English the music is of a limited nature. You've got Chaucer's French perfection, you've got Shakespeare's Italian perfection, you've got

Campion and Lawes. I don't think I got around to this kind of form until I got to the choruses in the *Trachiniae*. I don't know that I got to anything at all, really, but I thought it was an extension of the gamut. It may be a delusion. One was always interested in the implication of change of pitch in the union of *motz et son*, of the word and melody.

• • •

Interviewer: There is an academic controversy about your influence on Yeats. Did you work over his poetry with him? Did you cut any of his poems in the way you cut *The Waste Land*?

Pound: I don't think I can remember anything like that. I am sure I objected to particular expressions. Once out at Rapallo I tried for God's sake to prevent him from printing a thing. I told him it was rubbish. All he did was print it with a preface saying that I *said* it was rubbish.

I remember when Tagore had taken to doodling on the edge of his proofs, and they told him it was art. There was a show of it in Paris. "Is this art?" Nobody was very keen on these doodlings, but of course so many people lied to him.

As far as the change in Yeats goes, I think that Ford Madox Ford might have some credit. Yeats never would have taken advice from Ford, but I think that Fordie helped him, via me, in trying to get towards a natural way of writing.

Interviewer: Did anyone ever help you with your work as extensively as you have helped others? I mean by criticism or cutting.

Pound: Apart from Fordie, rolling on the floor undecorously and holding his head in his hands, and groaning on one occasion, I don't think anybody helped me through my manuscripts. Ford's stuff appeared too loose then, but he led the fight against tertiary archaisms.

Interviewer: You have been closely associated with visual artists—Gaudier-Brzeska and Wyndham Lewis in the vorticist movement, and later Picabia, Picasso, and Brancusi. Has this had anything to do with you as a writer?

Pound: I don't believe so. One looked at paintings in galleries and one might have found out something. "The Game of Chess" poem shows the effect of modern abstract art, but vorticism from my angle was a renewal of the sense of construction. Color went dead and Manet and the impressionists revived it. Then what I would call the sense of form was blurred, and vorticism, as distinct from cubism, was an attempt to revive the sense of form—the form you had in Piero della

Francesca's *De Prospettive Pingendi*, his treatise on the proportions and composition. I got started on the idea of comparative forms before I left America. A fellow named Poole did a book on composition. I did have *some* things in my head when I got to London, and I *had* heard of Catullus before I heard about modern French poetry. There's a bit of biography that might be rectified.

.   .   .

Interviewer: It is amazing that you could come to Europe and quickly associate yourself with the best living writers. Had you been aware of any of the poets writing in America before you left? Was Robinson anything to you?

Pound: Aiken tried to sell me Robinson and I didn't fall. This was in London too. I then dragged it out of him that there was a guy at Harvard doing funny stuff. Mr. Eliot turned up a year or so later.

No, I should say that about 1900, you had Carman and Hovey, Carwine and Vance Cheney. The impression then was that the American stuff wasn't *quite* as good as the English at any point. And you had Mosher's pirated editions of the English stuff. No, I went to London because I thought Yeats knew more about poetry than anybody else. I made my life in London by going to see Ford in the afternoons and Yeats in the evenings. By mentioning one to the other one could always start a discussion. That was the exercise. I went to study with Yeats and found that Ford disagreed with him. So then I kept on disagreeing with *them* for twenty years.

Interviewer: In 1942, you wrote that you and Eliot disagreed by calling each other protestants. I wonder when you and Eliot diverged.

Pound: Oh, Eliot and I started diverging from the beginning. The fun of an intellectual friendship is that you diverge on some thing or other and agree on a few points. Eliot, having had the Christian patience of tolerance all his life and so forth, and working very hard, must have found me very trying. We started disagreeing about a number of things from the time we met. We also agreed on a few things and I suppose both of us must have been right about something or other.

.   .   .

Interviewer: One point of connection between literature and politics which you make in your writing interests me particularly. In the *A.B.C. of Reading* you say that good writers are those who keep the language efficient, and that this is their function. You disassociate this function from party. Can a man of the wrong party use language efficiently?

Pound: Yes. That's the whole trouble! A gun is just as good, no matter who shoots it.

Interviewer: Can an instrument which is orderly be used to create disorder? Suppose good language is used to forward bad government? Doesn't bad government make bad language?

Pound: Yes, but bad language is *bound* to make in addition bad government, whereas good language is *not* bound to make bad government. That again is clear Confucius: if the orders aren't clear they can't be carried out. Lloyd George's laws were such a mess, the lawyers never knew what they meant. And Talleyrand proclaimed that they changed the meaning of words between one conference and another. The means of communication breaks down, and that of course is what we are suffering now. We are enduring the drive to work on the subconscious without appealing to the reason. They repeat a trade name with the music a few times, and then repeat the music without it so that the music will give you the name. I think of the *assault*. We suffer from the use of language to conceal thought and to withhold all vital and direct answers. There is the definite use of propaganda, forensic language, merely to conceal and mislead.

Interviewer: Where do ignorance and innocence end and the chicanery begin?

Pound: There is natural ignorance and there is artificial ignorance. I should say at the present moment the artificial ignorance is about eighty-five per cent.

• • •

Interviewer: The political action of yours that everybody remembers is your broadcasts from Italy during the war. When you gave these talks, were you conscious of breaking the American law?

Pound: No, I was completely surprised. You see I had that promise. I was given the freedom of the microphone twice a week. "He will not be asked to say anything contrary to his conscience or contrary to his duty as an American citizen." I thought that covered it.

Interviewer: Doesn't the law of treason talk about "giving aid and comfort to the enemy," and isn't the enemy the country with whom we are at war?

Pound: I thought I was fighting for a constitutional point. I mean to say, I may have been completely nuts, but I certainly *felt* that it wasn't committing treason.

Wodehouse went on the air and the British asked him not to. Nobody asked me not to. There was no announcement until the collapse that the people who had spoken on the radio would be prosecuted.

Having worked for years to prevent war, and seeing the folly of Italy and America being at war—! I certainly wasn't telling the troops to revolt. I thought I was fighting an internal question of constitutional government. And if any man, any individual man, can say he has had a bad deal from me because of race, creed, or color, let him come out and state it with particulars. The *Guide to Kulchur* was dedicated to Basil Bunting and Louis Zukovsky, a Quaker and a Jew.

I don't know whether you think the Russians ought to be in Berlin or not. I don't know whether I was doing any good or not, whether I was doing any harm. Oh, I was probably offside. But the ruling in Boston was that there is no treason without treasonable intention.

What I was right about was the conservation of individual rights. If, when the executive or any other branch exceeds its legitimate powers, no one protests, you will lose all your liberties. My method of opposing tyranny was wrong over a thirty-year period; it had nothing to do with the Second World War in particular. If the individual, or heretic, gets hold of some essential truth, or sees some error in the system being practiced, he commits so many marginal errors himself that he is worn out before he can establish his point.

The world in twenty years has piled up hysteria—anxiety over a third war, bureaucratic tyranny, and hysteria from paper forms. The immense and undeniable loss of freedoms, as they were in 1900, is undeniable. We have seen the acceleration in efficiency of the tyrannizing factors. It's enough to keep a man worried. Wars are made to make debt. I suppose there's a possible out in space satellites and other ways of making debt.

Interviewer: When you were arrested by the Americans, did you then expect to be convicted? To be hanged?

Pound: At first I puzzled over having missed a cog somewhere. I expected to turn myself in and to be asked about what I learned. I did and I wasn't. I know that I checked myself, on several occasions during the broadcasts, on reflecting that it was not up to me to do certain things, or to take service with a foreign country. Oh, it was paranoia to think one could argue against the usurpations, against the folks who got the war started to get America into it. Yet I hate the idea of obedience to something which is wrong.

Then later I was driven into the courtyard at Chiavari. They had been shooting them, and I thought I was finished then and there. Then finally a guy came in and said he was damned if he would hand me over to the Americans unless I wanted to be handed over to them.

Interviewer: In 1942, when the war started for America, I understand you tried to leave Italy and come back to the United States. What were the circumstances of the refusal?

Pound: Those circumstances were by hearsay. I am a bit hazy in my head about a considerable period, and I think that . . . I know that I had a chance to get as far as Lisbon, and be cooped up there for the rest of the war.

● ● ●

Interviewer: Are you more or less stuck?

Pound: Okay, I am stuck. The question is, am I dead, as Messrs. A.B.C. might wish? In case I conk out, this is provisionally what I have to do: I must clarify obscurities; I must make clearer definite ideas or dissociations. I must find a verbal formula to combat the rise of brutality—the principle of order versus the split atom. There was a man in the bughouse, by the way, who insisted that the atom had never been split.

An epic is a poem containing history. The modern mind contains heteroclite elements. The past epos has succeeded when all see a great many of the answers were assumed, at least between author and audience, or a great mass of audience. The attempt in an experimental age is therefore rash. Do you know the story: "What are you drawing, Johnny?"

"God."

"But nobody knows what He looks like."

"They will when I get through!"

That confidence is no longer obtainable.

There *are* epic subjects. The struggle for individual rights is an epic subject, consecutive from jury trial in Athens to Anselm versus William Rufus, to the murder of Becket and to Coke and through John Adams.

Then the struggle appears to come up against a block. The nature of sovereignty is epic matter, though it may be a bit obscured by circumstance. Some of this *can* be traced, pointed; obviously it has to be condensed to get into the form. The nature of the individual, the heteroclite contents of contemporary consciousness. It's the fight for light versus subconsciousness; it demands obscurities and penumbras. A lot of contemporary writing avoids inconvenient areas of the subject.

I am writing to resist the view that Europe and civilization are going to Hell. If I am being "crucified for an idea"—that is, the coherent idea around which my muddles accumulated—it is probably the idea that European culture ought to survive, that the best qualities of it ought to survive along with whatever other cultures, in whatever universality. Against the propaganda of terror and the propaganda of luxury, have you a nice simple answer? One has worked on certain materials trying to establish bases and axes of reference. In writing so as to be understood, there is always the problem of rectification without giving up what is correct. There is the struggle not to sign on the dotted line for the opposition.

Interviewer: Do the separate sections of the *Cantos*, now—the last three sections have appeared under separate names—mean that you are attacking particular problems in particular sections?

Pound: No. *Rock Drill* was intended to imply the necessary resistance in getting a certain main thesis across—hammering. I was not following the three divisions of the *Divine Comedy* exactly. One can't follow the Dantesquan cosmos in an age of experiment. But I have made the division between people dominated by emotion, people struggling upwards, and those who have some part of the divine vision. The thrones in Dante's *Paradiso* are for the spirits of the people who have been responsible for good government. The thrones in the *Cantos* are an attempt to move out from egoism and to establish some definition of an order possible or at any rate conceivable on earth. One is held up by the low percentage of reason which seems to operate in human affairs. *Thrones* concerns the states of mind of people responsible for something more than their personal conduct.

Interviewer: Now that you come near the end, have you made any plans for revising the *Cantos*, after you've finished?

Pound: I don't know. There's need of elaboration, of clarification, but I don't know that a comprehensive revision is in order. There is no doubt that the writing is too obscure as it stands, but I hope that the order of ascension in the Paradiso will be toward a greater limpidity. Of course there ought to be a corrected edition because of errors that have crept in.

Interviewer: Let me change the subject again, if I may. In all those years in St. Elizabeth's, did you get a sense of contemporary America from your visitors?

Pound: The trouble with visitors is that you don't get enough of the opposition. I suffer from the cumulative isolation of not having had enough contact—fifteen years living more with ideas than with persons.

Interviewer: Do you have any plans for going back to the States? Do you want to?

Pound: I undoubtedly want to. But whether it is nostalgia for America that isn't there any more or not I don't know. This is a difference between an abstract Adams–Jefferson–Adams–Jackson America, and whatever is really going on. I undoubtedly have moments when I should like very much to live in America. There are these concrete difficulties against the general desire. Richmond is a beautiful city, but you can't live in it unless you drive an automobile. I'd like at least to spend a month or two a year in the U.S.

Interviewer: You said the other day that as you grew older you felt more American all the time. How does this work?

Pound: It works. Exotics were necessary as an attempt at a foundation. One is transplanted and grows, and one is pulled up and taken back to what one has been transplanted from and it is no longer there. The contacts aren't there and I suppose one reverts to one's organic nature and finds it merciful. Have you ever read Andy White's memoirs? He's the fellow who founded Cornell University. That was the period of euphoria, when everybody thought that all the good things in America were going to function, before the decline, about 1900. White covers a period of history that goes back to Buchanan on one side. He alternated between being Ambassador to Russia and head of Cornell.

Interviewer: Your return to Italy has been a disappointment, then?

Pound: Undoubtedly. Europe was a shock. The shock of no longer feeling oneself in the center of something is probably part of it. Then there is the incomprehension, Europe's incomprehension, of organic America. There are so many things which I, as an American, cannot say to a European with any hope of being understood. Somebody said that I am the last American living the tragedy of Europe.

Part II

General Criticism

Marianne Moore

Teach, Stir the Mind, Afford Enjoyment[1]

Our debt to Ezra Pound is prodigious for the effort he has made to share what he knows about writing and, in particular, about rhythm and melody; most of all, for his insistence on liveness as opposed to deadness. "Make it new," he says. "Art is a joyous thing." He recalls "that sense of sudden growth we experience in the presence of the greatest works of art." The ode to *Hugh Selwyn Mauberley* applies of course to himself:

> For three years, out of key with his time,
> He strove to resuscitate the dead art
>
> Of poetry; to maintain "the sublime"
> In the old sense. . . .

And, above all, it is the art of letters in America that he has wished to resuscitate. He says in "Cantico del Sole":

> The thought of what America would be like
> If the classics had a wide circulation
>   Troubles my sleep. . . .

America's imperviousness to culture irks him; but he is never as indignant as he is elated.

Instruction should be painless, he says, and his precept for writers is

[1] From a series of commentaries on selected contemporary poets. Bryn Mawr, 1952.

an epitome of himself: teach, stir the mind, afford enjoyment. (Cicero's
Ut doceat, ut moveat, ut delectet.[2]) Hugh Kenner grants him his wish
and says: "The Pound letters are weirdly written; they are nevertheless
a treatise on creative writing, treasure-trove, *corpus aureum, mina de
oro.* . . . The vivacity of these letters is enchanting." Mr. Kenner also
says, "The whole key to Pound, the basis of his Cantos, his music, his
economics and everything else, is the concern for exact definition"—a
passion shared by T. S. Eliot, Mr. Kenner adds—"a quality which neither
has defined." What is it? a neatening or cleancutness, to begin with, as
caesura is cutting at the end (*caedo*, cut off). For Dante, it was making
you see the thing that he sees, Mr. Pound says; and, speaking of
Rimbaud, says there is "such firmness of coloring and such certitude."
Pound admires Chinese codifyings and for many a year has been ordering, epitomizing, and urging explicitness, as when he listed "A Few
Don'ts" for Imagists:

> Direct treatment, economy of words; compose in the sequence
> of the musical phrase rather than that of the metronome.
> The true poet is most easily distinguished from the false when he
> trusts himself to the simplest expression and writes without adjectives.
> No dead words or phrases.
> A thought should be expressed in verse at least as well as it could
> be expressed in prose. Great literature is language charged with
> meaning to the utmost possible degree. There is no easy way out.

Mr. Pound differentiates poetry as

> logopoeia (music of words),
> melopoeia (music of sound)—the music of rhymes, he says, depends
>   upon their arrangement, not only on their multiplicity—and
> phanopoeia (casting images on the imagination).

Under the last head, one recalls the statement by Dante that Beatrice
walked above herself—*come una crana.* Confucius says the fish moves
on winglike foot; and Prior, in his life of Edmund Burke, says Burke
"had a peculiarity in his gait that made him look as if he had two left
legs." Affirming Coleridge's statement that "Our admiration of a great

[2] See Kenneth Burke's "The Language of Poetry, 'Dramatistically' Considered,"
paper written for a symbolism seminar conducted in 1952-53 by the Institute for
Religious and Social Studies, New York (*Chicago Review*, Fall 1954): "We would
spin this discussion from Cicero's terms for the 'three offices of the orator.' (See
Orator, De Oratore, and St. Augustine's use of this analysis of Christian persua-
sion in his *De Doctrina Christiana*.) First office: to teach or inform *(docere)*.
Second Office: to please *(delectare)*. Third office: to move or 'bend' *(movere,
flectare)*."

poet is for a continuous undercurrent of feeling everywhere present, but seldom anywhere a separate excitement," Mr. Pound says Dante "has gone living through Hell and the words of his lament sob as branches beaten by the wind."

What is poetry? Dante said, "a song is a composition of words set to music." As for free verse, "it is *not* prose," Mr. Pound says. It is what we have "when the thing builds up a rhythm more beautiful than that of set metres"—as here:

> The birds flutter to rest in my tree,
>   and I think I have heard them saying,
> "It is not that there are no other men—,
> But we like this fellow the best. . . ."

In Dante, "we have blending and lengthening of the sounds, heavy beats," Mr. Pound says. "Don't make each line stop dead at the end. Let the beginning of the next line catch the rise of the rhythm wave, unless you want a longish definite pause." For example, the lines from "Envoi" in *Mauberley*, when he speaks of "her graces":

> I would bid them live
> As roses might, in magic amber laid,
> Red overwrought with orange and all made
> One substance and one colour
> Braving time.

This is the way in which to cement sound and thought. In *Mauberley*, also note the identical rhymes in close sequence without conspicuousness, or "Medallion":

> The face-oval beneath the glaze,
> Bright in its suave bounding-line, as,
> Beneath half-watt rays,
> The eyes turn topaz.

"Words," T. S. Eliot says, "are perhaps the hardest medium of all material of art. One must simultaneously express visual beauty, beauty of sound, and communicate a grammatical statement." We have in "her" a mundane word, but note the use made of it in Portrait, from "La Mère Inconnue" *(Exultations)*:

> Nay! For I have seen the purplest shadows stand
> Always with reverent chere that looked on her,
> Silence himself is grown her worshipper

> And ever doth attend her in that land
> Wherein she reigneth, wherefore let there stir
> Naught but the softest voices, praising her.

Again, from Ezra Pound's translation of Guido Cavalcanti: "A Bernardo da Bologna,"

> And in that Court where Love himself fableth
> Telling of beauties he hath seen, he saith:
> This pagan and lovely woman hath in her
> All strange adornments that ever were.

William Carlos Williams is right. "Pound is not 'all poetry.' . . . But he has an ear that is unsurpassable." "Some poems," Mr. Pound himself says, "have form as a tree has form and some as water poured into a vase." He also says, quoting Arnold Dolmetsch and Mace: "Mark not the beat too much"—a precept essential to light rhyme and surprises within the line; but inapplicable to satire, as in W. S. Gilbert's *Pirates of Penzance*—the policemen:

> And yet when someone's near
> We manage to appear
> As unsusceptible to fear
> As anybody here.

"The churn, the loom, the spinning-wheel, the oars," Mr. Pound says, "are bases for distinctive rhythm which can never degenerate into the monotony of mere iambs and trochees"; and one notices in "Nel Biancheggiar" the accenting of "dies," in "but dies not quite":

> I feel the dusky softness whirr
> Of Colour, as upon a dulcimer
>   .   .   .
> As when the living music swoons
> But dies not quite . . . .

One notes in "Guido Invites You Thus" *(Exultations)* the placing of the pauses and quickened "flames of an altar fire":

> Lo, I have known thy heart and its desire;
> Life, all of it, my sea, and all men's streams
> Are fused in it as flames of an altar fire!

And "A Prologue" *(Canzoni)* has the same exactitude in variety:

> Shepherds and kings, with lambs and frankincense
> Go and atone for mankind's ignorance:
> Make ye soft savour from your ruddy myrrh.
> Lo, how God's son is turned God's almoner.

Unending emphasis is laid by Ezra Pound on honesty—on voicing one's own opinion. He is indignant that "trout should be submerged by eels." The function of literature, he says, is "to incite humanity to continue living; to ease the mind of strain; to feed it" (Canto XXV):

> What we thought had been thought for too long;
>
> . . .
>
> We have gathered a sieve full of water.
>
> . . .
>
> The dead words, keeping form.

We suffer from

> Noble forms lacking life,
>
> . . .
>
> The dead concepts, never the solid;

As for the comprehension of what is set forth, the poet has a right to expect the reader, at least in a measure, to be able to complete the poetic statement; and Ezra Pound never spoils his effects by over-exposition. He alludes as follows to the drowning of a Borgia:

> The bust outlasts the shrine;
> The coin, Tiberius.
>
> . . .
>
> John Borgia is bathed
> at last. And the cloak floated.

"As for *Cathay*, it must be pointed out," T. S. Eliot says, "that Pound is the inventor of Chinese poetry of our time"; and seeing a connection between the following incident and "the upper-middlebrow press," Hugh Kenner recalls that when Charles Münch offered Bach to the regiment, the commandant said, "Here, none of that mathematical music." One ventures, commits one's self, and if readers are not pleased, one can perhaps please one's self and earn that slender right to persevere.

"A poet's work," Mr. Eliot says, "may proceed along two lines of an imaginary graph; one of the lines being his conscious and continuous effort in technical excellence," and the other "his normal human course of development. Now and then the two lines may converge at a high peak, so that we get a masterpiece. That is to say, an accumulation of experience has crystallized to form material of art, and years of work in technique have prepared an adequate medium; and something results in which medium and material, form and content, are indistinguishable."

In *The Great Digest and Unwobbling Pivot* of Confucius, as in his *Analects*, Ezra Pound has had a theme of major import. *The Great Digest* makes emphatic this lesson: He who can rule himself can govern others; he who can govern others can rule the kingdom and families of the Empire.

> The men of old disciplined themselves.
> Having attained self-discipline they set their houses in order.
> Having ordered in their own homes, they brought good government to their own state.
> When their states were well governed, the empire was brought into equilibrium.

We have in the *Digest*, content that is energetic, novel, and deep: "If there be a knife of resentment in the heart or enduring rancor, the mind will not attain precision; under suspicion and fear it will not form sound judgment, nor will it, dazzled by love's delight nor in sorrow and anxiety, come to precision." As for money, "Ill got, ill go." When others have ability, if a man "shoves them aside, he can be called a real pest." "The archer when he misses the bullseye, turns and seeks the cause of error in himself." There must be no rationalizing. "Abandon every clandestine egoism to realize the true root." Of the golden rule, there are many variants in the *Analects*: "Tze-kung asked if there was a single principle that you could practise through life to the end. He said sympathy; what you don't want, don't inflict on another" (Book Fifteen, XXIII). "Require the solid of yourself, the trifle of others" (Book Fifteen, XIV). "The proper man brings men's excellence to focus, not their evil qualities" (Book Twelve, XVI). "I am not worried that others do not know me; I am worried by my incapacity" (Book Fourteen, XXXII). Tze-chang asked Kung-tze about maturity. Kung-tze said: To be able to practise five things would humanize the whole empire—sobriety *(serenitas)*, magnanimity, sticking by one's word, promptitude (in attention to detail), kindliness *(caritas)*. As for "the problem of style. Effect your meaning. Then stop" (Book Fifteen, XL).

In "Salvationists," Mr. Pound says:

> Come, my songs, let us speak of perfection—
> We shall get ourselves rather disliked.

We shall get ourselves disliked and very much liked, because the zest for perfection communicates its excitement to others.

Hugh Kenner

The Muse in Tatters

The Sapphic fragment concerning Gongyla, which in 1916 yielded Pound his "Papyrus," is actually parchment, one of three such parchment scraps torn by good fortune from a book destroyed centuries ago, the kind of book into which especially precious things were transcribed because papyrus disintegrates. They were salvaged from among masses of illegible papyrus scraps that come to Berlin from Egypt in 1896. Professor Schubart six years later published in a German journal[1] the letters he could then make out, bits of three poems of Sappho's, and in 1907 a reconsidered deciphering[2] which by two years later (*Classical Review*, July 1909) J. M. Edmonds had reconsidered yet more fully. There we may find

ἦρ ἀ[.	[Spring . . . . .]
δῆρα τō[.	[Too long . . . . .]
Γογγύλα τ[.	[Gongula . . . .]

. . . plus parts of a dozen more lines, nine of which, the parchment scrap growing suddenly wider, contained enough more words and bits

[1] Professor Schubart published in a German journal: *Sitzungsberichte der Akademie der Wissenschaften*, 1902, pp. 195-206.
[2] A reconsidered deciphering: *Berliner Klassikertexte*, V-2.

From The Pound Era, *by Hugh Kenner (Berkeley and Los Angeles, Calif.: University of California Press, 1971). Footnoted and textual translations have been provided by the editor. Reprinted by permission of the Regents of The University of California.*

of words to tempt Prof. Edmonds' skill as an ancient Greek poet. He diligently "restored" them, and offered a confident translation into Wardour Street. ("I would fain have thee set me in the dewy meadow whither aforetime. . . .") Half the Greek words he was rendering were his own. In subsequent versions he grew still more confident, and the incautious user of his Loeb Classical Library Sappho (*Lyra Graeca*, Vol. 1, 245) has been likely to suppose the poem substantially intact. It is not; and a half-century later Pound's dry rendering of three words in the upper left corner Edmonds left untinkered with still displaces in the memory Edmonds' tushery. Which was part of what Pound meant.

. . .

Pound was alerted to the new fragments of Sappho by some verses Richard Aldington gave him not long after they first met in 1912. Aldington had rendered a poem "To Atthis (*After the Manuscript of Sappho now in Berlin*)," working from an Edmonds restoration in the June 1909 *Classical Review*, the issue before the one that offered Gongula. Pound sent the version to Harriet Monroe for her new magazine, but though she used three Aldington poems in the second number of *Poetry* she did not use "To Atthis," having taken the odd precaution of checking with the head of the Greek Department at the University of Chicago, almost as if she'd known the translator was a scant nineteen. And Paul Shorey, she wrote Pound (9 Nov. 1912), "wouldn't stand for it,"[3] and she thought it advisable not to antagonize the scholars. She considered Shorey "no mere dry-as-dust." Pound replied that the Greek was so mutilated no man living could talk of it in absolutes. "I'd like to see Shorey's translation of the sense of the thing as it stands. I don't agree with R's translation—but it is quite beautiful scholarship or no scholarship." Harriet did not budge. She believed Chicago scholars. Seven years later her belief in W. G. Hale was to terminate Pound's connection with the magazine. Pound for his part anthologized "To Atthis" in *Des Imagistes* (1914), and later reaffirmed his admiration in *The Egoist*: "Aldington's version of the Atthis poem, from J. M. Edmonds' conjectural restoration, will, I think, take its place in any 'complete' English 'Sappho' in the future."[4] Aldington never reprinted it. It remains part of the story. It took Pound to Greek fragments, to the files of the *Classical Review*, so to Gongula, and most important, to the poem Aldington had translated.

[3] Paul Shorey "wouldn't stand for it": letter and Pound's reply, unpublished, in Harriet Monroe Collection, Univ. of Chicago Library.
[4] Pound reaffirmed his admiration: *Egoist*, V (Nov.-Dec. 1918), p. 130.

Of this poem, from the same ruined book as the Gongula scrap, a larger piece of parchment preserves much more: a torn beginning,[5] a torn ending, and in between them five stanzas entire: a very notable addition to the Sapphic canon, in which one poem of seven stanzas, the "Poikilothron',"* and four stanzas of another, the "Phainetai moi" ["Methinks"] ,** had hitherto been the only substantial exhibits.

And its tone is elegiac. For a thousand years no more than four lines of Sappho's on such a theme had been accessible to anyone. To Pound, then intent on a poiesis of loss, it came punctually: a sustained lament for an absence, for the absence of a familiar of Sappho and Atthis, now among the girls of Lydia and remembered across the sundering sea. What we have of it is built around a long "Homeric" simile,[6] separately elaborated and keyed by the Homeric word βροδοδάκτυλος [rosy-fingered] , unique outside of Homer and unique in being applied to the moon, not in Homer's way to the dawn: "rosy-fingered." *Brododaktylos* is Sappho's spelling, the initial *b* a mark of her dialect; the word so spelled lodged itself in Pound's mind, not to be touched for 30 years, but in Pisa one day to help unlock word-hoards. The whole poem became, as soon as he discovered it, a nexus for the nuanced elegiacs he had been concerned with since he wrote *Cathay* and turned 30. Its few dozen words disclose Sappho who longs for a distant girl, and imagines her in turn longing for the Atthis whom Sappho's words address though she too may be absent, while a moon rosy-fingered, as pre-eminent among the stars as the distant girl among the girls of Lydia, shines on the salt sea at dusk and on the flowers. Most of the words concern the moon's remote lustrations; like "The Jewel Stairs' Grievance" of the 1915 *Cathay*, "the poem is especially prized because she utters no direct reproach."

Aldington's version ran:

> Atthis, far from me and dear Mnasidika,
> Dwells in Sardis;
> Many times she was near us
> So that we lived life well
> Like the far-famed goddess
> Whom above all things music delighted.

[5] A torn beginning: the standard edition is Lobel & Page, *Poetarum Lesbiorum Fragmenta*, 1955, #96, but quotations in this book are from the *Classical Review* version Pound used.

*First word of the ode to Aphrodite. *[ed. note]*

**Opening of Sappho's second ode. *[ed. note]*

[6] "Homeric" simile: see Phillip Damon, *Modes of Analogy in Ancient and Mediaeval Verse*, 1961, pp. 272-280.

And now she is first among the Lydian women
As the mighty sun, the rose-fingered moon,
Beside the great stars.

And the light fades from the bitter sea
And in like manner from the rich-blossoming earth;
And the dew is shed upon the flowers,
Rose and soft meadow-sweet
And many-coloured melilote.
Many things told are remembered of sterile Atthis.

I yearn to behold thy delicate soul
To satiate my desire. . . .

. . . .[7]

"The mighty sun" mangles a phrase meaning "after sunset" (de-
riving δύντος from δυνατός [powerful] instead of from δύνω [sink]),
and Atthis has become the absent girl rather than the girl addressed,
and toward the end a Gordian tangle which Edmonds explicates for half
a column has been most arbitrarily cut. And so on. It is clear why
Professor Shorey "wouldn't stand for it." The point in Pound's letter
to Miss Monroe remains valid: all editions from Schubart's of 1902 to
Lobel and Page's of 1955 wrestle in their fine print with the fact that
once we have passed the word "melilote" the parchment offers im-
penetrable riddles from which only rough sense is to be gleaned. This
part is worth examining; it will occupy us again. Edmonds' text read:

πόλλα δὲ ζαφοίταισ᾽ ἀγόνας ἐπι-
μνάσθεισ᾽ ᾽Ατθιδος, ἰμέρω
λεπταν ϝοι φρένα κῆρ ἄσαι βόρηται

which with some grammatical forcing he took to mean:

And oftentime when our beloved, wandering abroad, calls to mind
her gentle Atthis, the heart devours her tender breast with the pain
of longing.

The Greek words do, in a general way, hang together, though no one
is really sure what some of them are, nor, whatever they are, how to
parse them. At one point everyone has read ἀγάνας, "gentle," except
Edmonds, who read ἀγόνας but assumed it stood for ἀγάνας ("it may
well be the Aeolic form"); Aldington's "sterile" ignores this assump-

---

[7] Aldington's version: in *Des Imagistes*, 1914, p. 19.

tion, supplying the dictionary sense of the word ̇Edmonds printed.
(So later, in Canto 5, we find "Atthis, unfruitful.") Then there is
ἰμέρω, a Lesbian form of ἰμείρω, "I yearn." What part of speech is it?
We are in a syntactic quagmire whatever we decide. Edmonds makes
ἰμέρω a genitive, at the price of a postulated syntax Sappho herself
might have had trouble following. Aldington took it at its dictionary
value, as an indicative verb with λέπταν φρένα for its object: "I yearn
for thy delicate soul." That leaves all the preceding words to be
trowelled into another independent clause. And of the verb form
βόρηται [heavyhearted] one could only suppose in Edmonds' day that
it had something to do with eating: hence Aldington's ingenious "to
satiate my desire," reinforced by his assignment of ἄσαι to ἄω, satiate,
instead of δάω, hurt. (Usages in later papyri make it possible to derive
βόρηται differently, and talk of the heart being laden.)

So the words in the Aldington version are generally referrable to
something in the Greek he was working from. Of course he was trying
to write a poem, not resolve paleographic austerites. How far these
were from resolution as late as 1955 we can learn from the 700 words
of erudite shadowboxing on pages 91-2 of Professor Page's *Sappho
and Alcaeus.*

.   .   .

To take from Sappho what one can use for one's poems was a
tradition understood by Catullus and practiced by English poets ever
since, in the 19th century, there were accessible collections of her work
to take from.[8] The edition Pound was used to, Wharton's of 1885,
illustrates both the range of Romantic and Decadent indebtedness, and
the slightness of the canon before 20th-century work with papyri more
than doubled it. Wharton's book commences with what were in the
year of Pound's birth the only two substantial poems of Sappho, each
attended by a small cloud of English translations and imitations, from
Ambrose Philips to John Addington Symonds; whereafter Wharton can
do no more than display the thin scrapings of generations of scholars:
a few other single stanzas, some portions of stanzas, and many stray
lines, stray phrases, single words, cited by Alexandrian commentators
in passing illustration of meters, or of Aeolic forms (so that we know
how she would have spelled the word for carbonate of soda), or of
semantic oddments like *barmos* and *barbitos*, names of musical instru-

[8]Accessible collections: the first was Wolf's, 1733, but scholarly interest and
proliferated editions did not peak for another century.

ments. Tiny though they are, these Sapphic details can rub off on other writings like bits of red dye; Wharton gives dozens of instances, and we can easily extend his citations. Thus the barbitos, and the "Pierian roses" an anthologist preserved in the 6th century along with 27 words of their context, were both to find their way into Pound's *Mauberley*; her "golden-sandalled dawn," from a line quoted only to show how she misused an adverb, is fused with a glimpse of Pavlova in his "The Garret": her distich on Hesper the bringer-home, which we owe to one word a grammarian wanted to annotate, stirred successive chords a hundred years apart in *Don Juan* and in *The Waste Land*.

In glimpses as brief as these her presence lingers, like the afterimage of a face. Of one song there survives one line, as quoted by Hephaestion of Alexandria to exemplify a meter: Ἠράμαν μὲν ἔγω σέθεν, Ἄτθι, πάλαι ποτά: "I loved you once, Atthis, long ago": only that, but its pauses, its run of sounds, its tautly paced disclosure running through seven overlapping words—so slow is the rose to open—roused Swinburne into eight lines of slow-motion re-enactment:

> *I loved thee,*—hark, one tenderer note than all—
> *Atthis, of old time, once—*one low long fall,
> Sighing—one long low lovely loveless call,
> Dying—one pause in song so flamelike fast—
> *Atthis, long since in old time overpast—*
> One soft first pause and last.
> One,—then the old rage of rapture's fieriest rain
> Storms all the music-maddened night again.[9]

This is surely the champion expansion, a document of the sensibility to which Pound's generation fell heir: a whole rhapsodic strophe on how it felt to read one Greek line. Would Dr. Johnson have carried on so? Yet although the rhapsode was Swinburne, who was never at a loss for more words, the Greek is shaped by an impassioned craft antiquity as well as Romanticism found exceptional; and its theme, an evoked regret, will glow without circumstance, as will gold in the gloom, sumptuous, for attention to prolong; and the art of attending to radioactive moments, "simply," in Pater's phrase, "for those moments' sake," had preoccupied two English generations. A central tradition of 19th-century decadence, a hyperaesthesia prizing and feeding on ecstatic instants, fragments of psychic continuum, answered a poetry time had reduced to fragments and endorsed the kind of attention fragments exact if we are to make anything of them at all, a

[9]Swinburne's slow-motion re-enactment: in *Songs of the Springtides*, 1880.

gathering of the responsive faculties into the space of a tiny blue flame. Having collected its attention, however, the impulse of this tradition was to dilate on attention's object: to reduplicate, to amplify, to prolong; to transcribe as for Wagner's orchestra. Observe, analogously, the pre-Raphaelite cumbrousness of detail generated (1830) in Tennyson's mind by a Shakespearean name, "Mariana," and a Shakespearean phrase, "moated grange."

.   .   .

Pound's pedagogic bent was against such consequences of hyperaesthesia. In the summer of 1916 he had reduced "the whole art,"[10] for Iris Barry's benefit, to

> *a.* concision, or style, or saying what you mean in the fewest and clearest words.
> *b.* the actual necessity for creating or constructing something: of presenting an image, or enough images of concrete things arranged to stir the reader.

He also admitted "simple emotional statements of fact, such as 'I am tired,' or simple credos like 'After death there comes no other calamity'." But he left no room for rapture's fieriest rain to storm the music-maddened night again, and had Swinburne's verses been submitted anonymously he would very likely have cut them back to the phrases on which they dilate. He prized Sappho for just the concision Swinburne obliterated, and to illustrate the chisel-edge of exactness drew Miss Barry's attention[11] to "the gulph between TIS O SAPPHO ADIKEI, and Pindar's big rhetorical drum TINA THEON, TIN' EROA, TINA D'ANDREA KELADESOMEN,"* misspelling words with the freedom of one who has them by heart. Τίς ἀδικήει: "Who wrongs you?": the question Aphrodite is to ask, in the 'Poikilothron'," when she comes to Sappho's aid: the sharp words of the goddess. (They are quoted in the *Pisan Cantos* and directed toward Athena, in a curious detail (76/461:490) which glimpses the descending Aphrodite in the guise of a butterfly that changes its mind and goes back out the tent's smoke hole.)

In the months in which he was writing to Iris Barry he was struggling to make Elkin Mathews print intact the sharp words of *Lustra*,

---

[10] Reduced "the whole art": *Letters*, #103.
[11] Drew Miss Barry's attention: *Letters*, #104.
*From an ode of Pindar's, quoted for sound rather than sense. *[ed. note]*

and one of the poems at which Mathews and his printer balked was
" Ἱμέρρω" [I long] ,[12] an extrapolation from a detail in the poem
Aldington had translated.[13] It says what it means in the fewest and
clearest words, and was eventually omitted from the British trade edition of *Lustra*. It extrapolates not by pouring Swinburne's hot fudge
over crystals of ice but by growing a larger crystal: supplying a phrase
with a structure. The phrase is Ἀτθίδος, ἰμέρω: for Atthis, longing.
Pound's expansion is

> Ἱμέρρω
> Thy soul
> Grown delicate with satieties,
> Atthis,
>
> O Atthis
> I long for thy lips.
> I long for thy narrow breasts,
> Thou restless, ungathered.

—a corrective to the music-maddened night, which Pound certainly
knew because Wharton's *Sappho* puts it on display.

He drew hints from two lines of Aldington's:

> I yearn to behold thy delicate soul
> To satiate my desire.

And since φρήν [mind, heart] designates the breast as well as the passion therein, he may have gotten the hint for "narrow breasts" from
the same phrase that suggested Aldington's "delicate soul." In the
course of inventing a poetic structure anything in the penumbra of
the poet's attention may suggest a word: even a page of the *Classical
Review* looked at sideways.

[12] Since the folk of Lesbos dropped their aitches this word takes a smooth
breathing, and did in three *Lustra* printings. The rough breathing it acquired in
the 1926 *Personae* and wore through four decades of reprints is traceable to a
misprint in the Concise Liddell and Scott *Lexicon*, where Pound had the bad
luck to check it. There are endless pitfalls in printing single Greek words; one
must imagine a compositor matching mirror images from an unfamiliar font
against queer things handwritten into a typescript: hence, throughout the Pound
canon, a tendency of accents to get reversed, and of similar shapes—Υ and γ,
ϛ and ξ, to get confused. And Pound generally did not use modern editions, but
the 18th-century ones he could pick up on bookstalls. And in Pisa he quoted
from unreliable memory.

[13] Mathews and his printer balked: see Forrest Read, ed., *Pound/Joyce*, 1967,
Appendix A, and Gallup, item A-11.

In *Lustra*, moreover, this is not an isolated poem but one of a suite of five poems. So we discover the point of "Papyrus," which Pound never printed by itself, for "Papyrus"—

> Spring . . . .
> Too long . . . . . .
> Gongula . . . .

—is the first poem of the suite, its authentic (mock authentic?) keynote. It is followed by

"IONE, DEAD THE LONG YEAR"

> Empty are the ways,
> Empty are the ways of this land
> And the flowers
> Bend over with heavy heads.
> They bend in vain.
> Empty are the ways of this land
> Where Ione
> Walked once, and now does not walk
> But seems like a person just gone.

The flowers and the absence are from Sappho, the girl's name from Landor, who devised it as a fine pseudonym for a Miss Jones. The third poem is "Ἰμέρρω." The fourth, which abandons the classical key, is

SHOP GIRL

> For a moment she rested against me
> Like a swallow half blown to the wall,
> And they talk of Swinburne's women,
> And the shepherdess meeting with Guido.
> And the harlots of Baudelaire.

—another girl now remembered in absence, but one never properly present: molecule of the merest encounter, "like a swallow half blown to the wall": yet a muse as were the women in other poets' perhaps imaginary encounters: and she was real. And nearly nonexistent: and granted no favors: and granted the stuff of a tiny poem, to set beside Guido Cavalcanti's five strophes[14]—*E tanto vi sentio gioi' e dolzore . . .* [I felt so much joy and sweetness]. Likewise in *Mauberley* a few years later the eyes of the eternal Aphrodite will look through the blank

[14]Cavalcanti's five strophes: *Translations*, pp. 116-117.

face of a London girl, being painted by Burne-Jones as a beggar-maid.
From a scrap of parchment with Gongyla's name on it the sequence
has traced modes of passion declining to this. For coda it paraphrases
Catullus' estimate of a comparable decline, which ends:

> And they call you beautiful in the province,
> And you are even compared to Lesbia.
>
> O most unfortunate age!

Pound has fitted Sappho, as he fits everything that interests him, into
an historical process, complicating the ancient tradition of poetic
aemulatio [emulation] with his own concern for cultural gradations.
It is 1916. The Cantos will before long be working in this way, setting
like beside almost like, to delineate losses and gains, new delicacies,
lost intensities.

.   .   .

In 1919, working on Canto 5, he returned to the poem about
Atthis and the absent girl, and once more spun filaments toward the
world of Catullus. The theme is passion, passion eventually flowing
(Borgia, Medici) into ideology and toward murder. The canto opens
with the bride awaiting the god's touch (Danaë, showered with gold)
and spirals through modes of love barely recapturable from time's
phantasmagoria:

> The fire? always, and the vision always,
> Ear dull, perhaps, with the vision, flitting
> And fading at will. Weaving with points of gold,
> Gold-yellow, saffron . . .

—from which shower of discriminated yellows (modulation of the
golden shower) a Roman wedding party emerges, Aurunculeia's, the
one celebrated by Catullus *(Carmen 61)*, with its saffron shoe crossing
the threshold, its flung nuts ("Da nuces"), its Hymenaeus:

> . . . The roman shoe, Aurunculeia's
> And come shuffling feet, and cries "Da nuces!
> "Nuces!" praise, and Hymenaeus "brings the girl to her man."

From this marriage we are carried to Sapphic love via two other poems,
Catullus' other epithalamion *(Carmen 62)* which begins "Vesper adest"
and proceeds under the sign of that star, and the distich of Sappho's

that begins "(H)espere panta pherōn" and has left its impress on work of Byron's, Tennyson's, Eliot's. Pound specifies only the link, the name of the star:

> and from "Hesperus . . ."
> Hush of the older song:

—and the "older song" is then paraphrased from words on the Berlin parchment.

Yet its most memorable feature is absent, its rich center, the Homeric simile Sappho built from the phrase about the rosy-fingered moon. Pound denied himself even the splendid word *brododaktylos*, apparently because it bespoke Homer too insistently to be usable. Catullus and Sappho were his terms of reference, and later privations and troubadours, but nothing epic. So he worked his way around *brododaktylos*, recalling that moons of that color, like the apparition of Hesper, occur at dusk, and gathered with Aldington's encouragement from *phaos* [daylight] in the tenth line[15] and *thalassan* [sea] in the eleventh the elements of

> "Fades light from sea-crest

In the seventh and eighth lines he found

> νῦν δὲ Λύδαισιν ἐμπρέπεται γτναί-
> κεσσιν

—"now she stands out among Lydian women"—and was very likely misled by the -ιυ termination of an Aeolic dative plural in which, perhaps distracted by a note of Edmonds' on νώιν, he fancied he saw a dual:

> "And in Lydia walks with pair'd women
> "Peerless among the pairs, . . .

Then . . .] Σαρδε [Sardis] [. . . (the last letter conjectural) from the very top of the parchment, the sole surviving token of its line if we disregard Edmonds' contributions, prompted a reticent ellipsis:

> . . . that once in Sardis

---

[15]In the tenth line: i.e., by Edmonds' numbering, which counts a hypothetical opening line he supplied. Aldington picked up the name "Mnasidika" from it.

—haunting poetry though obscure geography, since Sardis is situated
in Lydia, not here where Sappho stands. And finally the sixteenth and
seventeenth lines, where Atthis is mentioned—

> πόλλα δὲ ζαφοίταισ' ἀγόνας ἐπι-
> μνάσθεισ' Ἄτθιδος, ἰμέρω

gave him, not without effort his summation. To the troublesome
declension and wide idiomatic applicability of the first of these words
Liddell and Scott devote two columns; on the possible syntax of the
third Edmonds (1909) expended some 300 words and Page (1955)
twice as many, to the effect that the sense is "often going to and fro,
she remembers gentle Atthis with yearning." Aldington had already
made ἰμέρω begin a new sentence. Pound plunged in, and, prompted
by Aldington, began by taking πόλλα not as "often" but as a neuter
plural, "many things." Given this assumption ζαφοίταισ' (= διαφοιτάω,
to roam about continually) yielded no sense; whereas two words later
the *Lexicon* supplies διαφορέω, to spread abroad, which given the
peculiarities of the Lesbian dialect he may have thought a plausible
emendation. Then ἐπιμνάσθεισ' yielded "brought to mind," whence:

> . . . and many things
> "Are set abroad and brought to mind of thee."

And to this result:

> Titter of sound about me, always.
>   and from "Hesperus . . ."
> Hush of the older song: "Fades light from sea-crest,
> "And in Lydia walks with pair'd women
> "Peerless among the pairs, that once in Sardis
> "In satieties . . .
>   Fades the light from the sea, and many things
> "Are set abroad and brought to mind of thee,"
> And the vinestocks lie untended, new leaves come to the shoots,
> North wind nips on the bough, and seas in heart
> Toss us chill crests
>   And the vine stocks lie untended
> And many things are set abroad and brought to mind
> Of thee, Atthis, unfruitful. . . .

"Hush of the older song," and here first audible in English: the
first considerable poem of Sappho's to be recovered since the printing

of Longinus' treatise in 1554 put in circulation the "Phainetai moi" Catullus had imitated. Only a few of its words are used as seed-crystals in *Lustra*, a few of its other words in Canto 5. Fragments of a fragment grow into radiant gists; it is in keeping with the kind of attention Sappho's Greek commands of an early 20th-century intelligence that Pound nowhere presents what we have of the poem entire.

.   .   .

Swinburne's scholarship was incomparably more exact (he could correct Jowett: "Another howler, Master!") but his sense of diction less highly developed. That is one measure not simply of the difference between two poets but of a change of characteristic sensibility between Swinburne's time and Pound's. When Eliot speaks of Byron's "imperceptiveness to the English word—so that he has to use a great many words before we become aware of him" he posits his own time's criteria.[16]

In any age how to read and how to write are complementary terms, and the reading of the Pound Era, like its writing, discerns patterns of diction and gathers meaning from non-consecutive arrays. We can tell one page of *Ulysses* from another at a glance; to our grandfathers they would have seemed as featureless as pages from a telephone directory. The Joyce of a famous anecdote spent hours rearranging fifteen words, but knew from the start what each of the words was to be. Sensitivity to detailed sculptured forms makes tolerable—cherishable—in our museums fragments a former generation would have eked out with more plaster than there is marble. "Points define a periphery," wrote Pound in 1950, and in 1965 a translator of Sappho[17] offered, where parchment is wholly ruined, neither a despairing blank nor a mosaic of conjectures but this:

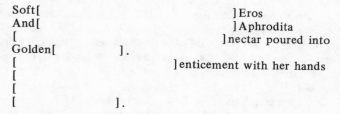

```
Soft[                          ]Eros
And[                           ]Aphrodita
[                              ]nectar poured into
Golden[           ].
[                         ]enticement with her hands
[
[
[              ].
```

16Eliot on Byron: in *On Poetry and Poets*, 1957, p. 201.
17A translator of Sappho: see Guy Davenport, *Sappho: Poems and Fragments*, 1965, poem 43.

```
[                        ] in the month of Geraistos
[                                    ] lovers
[                                    ] never
[            ] I shall come.
```

That the name of a month, and "lovers" and "never," and the resolve
to come are discoverable in each other's neighborhood is to us an expressive fact, helping to characterize the ruined stanza. Similar skills
brought to bear on torn pages would assure us that

```
            ] banyan, frangipani or
          ] s; or an exotic serpent
          ] and snake-skin for the foot, if you see fit,
        ] cats, not cobras to
        ] he rats. The diffident      [
```

is by Marianne Moore and not Ezra Pound, and that

```
            ] make price[
          ] teste leopard        [
          ] Taormina                    [
        ]  high cliff and azure beneath it[
        ] in the lute's neck, tone is from the b[
        ] s alone over Selloi                      [
          ] This wing, colour of feldspar    [
              ]                    phylotaxis      [
```

is by Ezra Pound and not Marianne Moore, and that neither can be a
scrap of William Carlos Williams.

Pound's attention, similarly, tended to fix on the constellated
words in ancient texts, not on their syntactic connections. He has
even suggested that preoccupation with reproducing syntax may get
in the translator's way, that Aeschylus' Greek is nearly agglutinative.[18]
In 1912 he conjectured that Arnaut Daniel might have evolved Moncli
and Audierna,[19] two lovers of whom nothing else is known, from two
passages misread in Vergil's ninth eclogue, Moncli being Menalcas
glimpsed through scribes' contractions, and Audierna a form of the
verb *audio* [hear] mistaken for a name, and the whole translated
"without too much regard for Latin syntax, with which Arnaut would
have been much less familiar than he was with the Latin vocabulary."

[18] Aeschylus nearly agglutinative: *LE*, p. 273.
[19] Moncli and Audierna: *Translations*, p. 424.

Pound has gone through such processes himself, not always unconsciously.

It is tenable that he saw diction rather than syntax because not having learned declensions accurately he could not follow the syntax. This is very likely often true, but does not itself explain why a man who was never lazy, and had an appetite for old poems, did not feel an incentive to perfect his grammatical knowledge. That he was impatient with people who possessed such knowledge is not an explanation but something else to explain. What did he know that they didn't? Which means, since a man will not willingly pore over what is opaque to him, what was he responding to when he read Greek? To rhythms and dictions, nutriment for his purposes. Especially in Greek lyrics he is sensitive to the boundaries of individual words, and apt to discern a talismanic virtue in relevant English words of his discovery. In the rare plural "satieties" he found a Sapphic quality concentrated. It appears in " Ἰμέρρω," it is cherished and carefully laminated into the fifth *Canto*, and we learn nothing of its virtue from knowing that it was prompted by Aldington's misreading of ἄσαι. It suffices that Pound came upon it in the rich field of his English vocabulary, and cherished it as affording a mysterious glimpse into intensities important to Sappho.

The five poems in *Lustra*, the lines in Canto 5, may be taken in this way detail by detail as exempla of the disciplined attention at work, attention disciplined not only by fragments of Greek but by a time's aesthetic, an aesthetic of glimpses. For the second Renaissance that opened for classicists in 1891 with a shower of papyri was a renaissance of attention. Perhaps nothing else ultimately matters in the arts. And like the Grand Renaissance it was long preparing before anyone suspected it was happening. Degas and Toulouse-Lautrec show us glimpses, comparable to

> For a moment she rested against me
> Like a swallow half blown to the wall.

The eye's shutter captures faces and gestures of the café or the street, so composed as to seem casual. Elsewhere Rossetti—

> A sonnet is a moment's monument,—
> Memorial from the Soul's eternity
> To one dead deathless hour

—and Pater—

Who, in some such perfect moment, . . . has not felt the desire to perpetuate all that, just so, to suspend it in every particular circumstance, with the portrait of just that one spray of leaves lifted just so high against the sky, above the well, forever?[20]

—adumbrate the metaphysics of the glimpse. Arthur Symons, the art of whose ideal poet Verlaine was "a delicate waiting upon moods," describes himself (1905)

as one who devoutly practiced "the religion of the eyes," looking into every omnibus, watching faces in the crowds which passed him in Piccadilly lest he miss a sudden gracious gesture, a beautiful face. . . . This was also the pleasure that the music-halls gave him: back-stage especially he enjoyed, like Degas, the vision of a world in flux—moving shapes and shadows; sudden unreal glimpses of the dancers on stage; profiles of the spectators. And if he watched carefully, the flux might momentarily resolve itself into an arrangement.[21]

To fix the last fine shade, said Symons, "to fix it fleetingly; to be a disembodied voice, and yet the voice of a human soul . . ."; and Pound accordingly not only preserves things glimpsed "In a Station of the Metro" or "Dans un Omnibus de Londres"—

Lex yeux d'une morte
M'ont salué,
Enchassés dans une visage stupide
Dont tous les autres traits étaient banals,
Ils m'ont salué

—but also echoes the presiding doctrines in "Horae Beatae Inscriptio"—

How will this beauty, when I am far hence
Sweep back upon me and engulf my mind!

—or in the little epigraph to *Lustra*:

And the days are not full enough
And the nights are not full enough
And life slips by like a field mouse
Not shaking the grass.

[20]Who, in some such perfect moment: quoted in Barbara Charlesworth, *Dark Passages*, 1965, p. 44.
[21]As one who devoutly practiced: Charlesworth, p. 110.

He echoes them however not in weariness, the note of Symons and Pater, but in a passionate generosity of attention; they were not canons of living but criteria for poems. When "each moment," as Pater wrote, "some tint grows more perfect on land or sea," then not to fix such perfections is "to sleep before evening." Let us die finely; our life is a long dying, amid which to be conscious is to capture melancholy satisfactions. No, let us write finely, Pound's concern rather ran, if it is our vocation to write, and seize moments in our writing, seize glimpses, there to seize, real: meanwhile

> Nothing but death, said Turgenev (Tiresias)
>   is irreparable.[22]

.   .   .

Pound was most deeply entangled in the aesthetic of glimpses in the *Lustra-Mauberley* period, the years when the elements of his mature method were being worked out. It is a period of looking back a little wistfully, a period of laments for departed experience, the period inaugurated by *Cathay*. Sappho, her fragments, her crystalline single words, remained bound up in his mind with this time, and with its end she drops out of his zone of preoccupation. By 1920 the fifth canto was in print, and the aesthetic of Paterian elegy which its first page recalls, the aesthetic he had exorcised in *Mauberley*, was replaced by the studied aesthetic of "hard squares" worked out under the sign of Fenollosa. In the 1920's, making reading lists for young students, he cited "of the Greeks, Homer, Sappho," and in the 1930's he set Mary Barnard to writing Sapphics ("have a care against spondee too often for second foot"[23]), but the explicit use of Sappho in his work remained confined to those late London years and their cultivated regrets: *Lustra*, Canto 5, *Mauberley*.

Then suddenly after a quarter-century circumstances changed the tone of the *Cantos* once more to elegy, and Sappho returned.

Irreparable death hung over the poet's head, and there were no books but Legge's Confucius and a Bible, and no sights but guards and prisoners and a sky and mountains and dust, and the *Pisan Cantos* invoked memory, seizing moments from the past "for those moments' sake." It was then that, reaching back to the time when Pound had pored over Greek fragments, memory yielded up, strangely, the splendid word of Sappho's that Canto 5 had skirted: *brododaktylos*. The

[22]Nothing but death: 80/494:527.
[23]"Have a care against spondee": *Letters*, #281.

word presented itself amid a sense that his own personality was dissolving into recollections. "To such a tremulous wisp constantly reforming itself on the stream, to a single sharp impression, with a sense in it, a relic more or less fleeting, of such moments gone by, what is real in our life fines itself down": so Pater had written in 1868, and so Pound felt in the summer of 1945. His mind ran on devouring Time, on the dead Ignez da Castro who brought the phrase "time is the evil" into the *Cantos*, on a woman's face remembered as though "dead the long year," on Mauberley's effort to memorialize such glimpses, working as Pisanello had worked on medallions in the Greek manner "to forge Achaia"; on new-made Aphrodite blown upon by winds; and on Aubrey Beardsley, doomed. And did he remember that Beardsley had designed the cover for the third printing of Wharton's *Sappho*?

> Time is not, Time is the evil, beloved
> Beloved the hours βροδοδάκτυλος
>   as against the half-light of the window
>   with the sea beyond making horizon
> le contre-jour the line of the cameo
> profile "to carve Achaia"
>   a dream passing over the face in the half-light
>   Venere, Cytherea "aut Rhodon"
>   vento ligure, veni
> "beauty is difficult" sd/ Mr Beardsley . . .
>   (74/444:472)

So Canto 74; and though the lament for a lost woman in a lost time accords with Sappho's theme, and the vocation of Beardsley and H. S. Mauberley with the sensibility of a time when fragments had seemed especially radiant, though Sappho's word thus bridges the two motifs of this passage, the fact should be recorded that in 1949 Pound could not say why he had used the Aeolic rather than the Homeric form of the word "rosy-fingered."[24] No matter: memory at the time of writing had supplied what was appropriate, and supplied it again in Canto 80 when amid memories of those London days Aubrey Beardsley's saying again drew up with it the Greek polysyllable:

> La beauté, "Beauty is difficult, Yeats" said Aubrey Beardsley
>   when Yeats asked why he drew horrors
>   or at least not Burne-Jones
>   and Beardsley knew he was dying and had to
>   make his hit quickly

[24]In 1949 Pound could not say: conversation with HK.

hence no more B-J in his product.

So very difficult, Yeats, beauty so difficult.

"I am the torch" wrote Arthur "she saith"
in the moon barge βροδοδάκτυλος Ἠώς [rosy-fingered dawn]

with the veil of faint cloud before her
Κύθηρα δεινά [terrible Aphrodite] as a leaf borne in the
current pale eyes as if without fire.

(80/511:546)

It is a poignant cluster: Beardsley; Arthur Symons, whose "Modern Beauty" began,

I am the torch, she saith, and what to me
If the moth die of me?

Κύθηρα δεινά, remembering perhaps Yeats' "terrible beauty"; her as-if-fireless pale eyes those of the moon (and perhaps of Agostino di Duccio's triumphant Diana in the Tempio at Rimini); the moon like Sappho's moon rosy-fingered, and rosy fingers specifying Homer's dawn.

The writer of those lines was living like Beardsley in the shadow of death, like Symons and Pater in the consciousness of a transience whose term is death, and as never before in his life was building with precious fragments, conserved by memory as the letters on parchments were conserved by chance: conserved for imaginations quickened by transience to scrutinize and irradiate. When he used Sappho's fragment on Atthis in 1916 it was as a means of writing elegiac poems, the elegy being the poetic genre his time gave him, a gift that corresponded to one of the moods of youth in that decade. When she returned to him in 1945, as it were anonymously, so that later he did not know that it was she and not Homer who had brought him a magical word, she re-enacted a rite celebrated by Symons and Yeats, assuming the guise of external Aphrodite who visits poets and whose gaze confers a sad ecstasy. Aphrodite comes in mean vestments, the myth runs: in the rags of the girl who posed for Burne-Jones's beggar-maid, or in a scrap of parchment.

Sister Bernetta Quinn

The Poet as Preceptor

If a reader regards Pound's *The Cantos* as too formidable an introduction to his poetry, he can begin with the highly readable prose. Here the writer very often assumes the role of preceptor, a word stemming from *praecipire*, "to know beforehand," and, as applied to Pound, meaning one who promulgates working rules respecting the techniques of an art. The rationale of all that he has written is contained in his critical essays, a factor which renders them decidedly useful to one who wants to know Pound. Moreover, his ideas are so influential that they have changed the character of four decades in American letters, have truly given poems (as the name of his New York publishing house suggests) new directions.

Some years ago, a young Irish poet, Malachy Quinn, picked up a volume of Pound's criticism in the British Museum, knowing nothing of the author. He went on to the early poems, the translations, and finally the *Cantos*, each step throwing its light into the subsequent area. His experience is an encouragement to all other serious students of modern literature, whether or not they be fellow craftsmen (like Quinn), who constitute the audience Pound had primarily in mind when he wrote his articles, later collected into book form, or his books planned as such from their inception.

From Ezra Pound: An Introduction to the Poetry, *by Sister Bernetta Quinn (New York and London: Columbia University Press, 1972). Reprinted by permission of the author, Columbia University Press and New Directions Publishing Corporation.*

Pound himself in his early years considered his criticism more a form of rhetoric than a lasting genre of appraisal. T. S. Eliot, who edited Pound's essays in 1954, felt otherwise: he states his purpose in reprinting the pieces in these words:

> . . . to regard the material in historical perspective, to put a new generation of readers, into whose hands the earlier collections and scattered essays did not come when they were new, into a position to appreciate the central importance of Pound's critical writing in the development of poetry during the first half of the twentieth century.[1]

Despite the absence of any evaluation of drama, no critic of our time, Eliot believes, can less be spared. He stresses the need to bear in mind the contexts in which the selections were written, none being produced in a vacuum or as ultimate; rather each is a landmark in the growth of a great sensibility. William Carlos Williams is at times credited with being the father of contemporary American poets. Never enthusiastic about Williams, Eliot takes a different position, calling Pound more responsible for the twentieth-century revolution in poetry than any other individual.[2] Pound's prose is much more lively than that of any other poet-critic of his age, brimming over as it is with apothegm, image, wit.

One of the greatest services Pound has done is to revive neglected authors, a service accompanied by attacks on established reputations if their makers have overshadowed finer men. His statements (sometimes pontifications) have weight in that he is never merely a theorist. He is capable of doing as well as of saying. Eliot praises the way in which Pound closes the gap between ideal and artifact:

> And of no other poet can it be more important to say that his criticism and his poetry, his precept and his practice, compose a single *oeuvre*. It is necessary to read Pound's poetry to understand his criticism and to read his criticism to understand his poetry.[3]

My belief in the truth of Eliot's assertion accounts for the inclusion of a discussion of Pound as preceptor in the present book.

The author of *The Waste Land* had good reason to extol Pound's critical acumen, as was revealed in November of 1968 when the unearthing in the New York Public Library vaults of the long-sought-for

---

[1] *The Literary Essays of Ezra Pound*, p. x.
[2] *Ibid*., p. xi.
[3] *Ibid*., p. xiii.

original manuscript, blue penciled by E.P., was widely publicized. *Time* magazine on that occasion juxtaposed Pound's gifts as a teacher and as a critic by captioning Wyndham Lewis's sketch of him "the ferrule of the teacher."[4] Later, *Time*'s feature writer said of the operations on *The Waste Land*: "A kind of miracle happened: the ferrule of the teacher became the poet's magic wand."[5]

In "Date Line," Pound separates criticism as he conceives it into five categories: (*a*) by discussion, as in Dante's *De Vulgari Eloquentia*, (*b*) by translation, (*c*) by imitation of a style, (*d*) by way of music, as he illustrates in his two operas based on the poets Villon and Cavalcanti, and (*e*) by new composition.[6] He then proceeds to divide its uses into the thought-process immediately prefacing creation (a benefit for artists only) and excernment, an unusual word which might broadly be understood as "seeing into" and in a narrower sense as "editing." The Latinate term derives from a search for a new way of speaking about criticism, for Pound an art meant for sifting out what is most valuable in the recorded *Sagetrieb* ("tale of the tribe"). On a more profound level, criticism, in his view, aims at making some contribution toward a *paideuma*, or culture, by the discovery of relationships among certain literary phenomena, leading to a body of knowledge necessary for the substructure of a cultured society.[7]

Many anthologists of criticism or historians of this branch of literature tend to exclude Pound, perhaps as a result of taking too literally his "Let it stand that the function of criticism is to efface itself when it has established its dissociations."[8] The fact is that these dissociations have to be established again and again if "the tale of the tribe" is to be told in purified, precise, vigorous language. Moreover, certain of Pound's essays, such as "A Few Don'ts for Imagistes," have become classics that no one has any wish to obliterate and that continue to affect the writing of poetry, just as they did at the time of their first publication.

Pound himself has never been much given to reading criticism, partly because of his dislike for abstractions, which inevitably predominate in such writing. Among his personal books, he has kept Eliot's critical essays, since these were the gifts of a friend. Another rather rare sign of interest in the theoretical is his retention of *The Name and Nature of Poetry* by A. E. Housman, which he marked up in the thirties

[4]November 22, 1968, p. 96.
[5]*Ibid.*
[6]*The Literary Essays of Ezra Pound*, pp. 74-75.
[7]*Ibid.*, p. 78.
[8]*Ibid.*, p. 80

and on which he wrote an article. His co-poets in English, however, both famous and obscure, are well represented in his private collection: Browning, Meredith, Crabbe, Beddoes, Byron, Wordsworth, Denham, the early balladeers, Coleridge, Armstrong, Dyer, Green, Beattie, Blair, Falconer, Church, Yeats, Moore (Marianne), Joyce, Manning, Eliot, H.D., Bunting, Ford. Most of these names turn up sooner or later in what he wrote, since we usually want to share what we love.

Pound's enthusiasms are so pervasive and so affirmatively proclaimed that a half-century of intellectually curious men and women have followed down the pathways of those interests he has opened up to them. In the preface to his 1910 edition of *The Spirit of Romance* he says: "The history of literature is hero-worship."[9] In addition to the heroes enshrined in the *Cantos*, Pound acquaints the reader of his criticism with such figures as Lucius Apuleius, Saint Francis Bernadone, François Villon, Lope de Vega. Everyone knows of his passion for the twelfth-century Arnaut Daniel, whose *maestria* was praised by Dante in the phrase which Eliot applies to Pound: *il miglior fabbro*, or "the better craftsman." Many of these literary interests he owes to the inspired teacher of his Hamilton days, William P. Shepard, who brought him through the rudiments of French, Italian, Spanish, and Provençal verse of the medieval period. Later the Lope de Vega expert Hugo Rennert, at the University of Pennsylvania, furthered his bent for translation and for critical essays. In the pursuit of his de Vega studies, Pound took all of southern Europe for his classroom and became more qualified each day to act as cicerone through the beginnings of Rennaissance literature.

From the winters of 1913 to 1916, when even the great William Butler Yeats looked upon his secretary in the little Sussex stone cottage as preceptor, to the present era of neo-Romantics, Pound's *magisterium* has been revered. Several generations of writers have found in his prose the example of a critic who knows what poems he likes and can tell why in a way that sustains original creative action. For over thirty years he held one "workshop" after another in his various apartments from London to Paris to Rapallo, or he conducted seminars of art theory in the restaurants he frequented in these places. When he retired from the capital of France to the relative obscurity of a small Italian beach town, he continued to be dominated by one passion: "And gladly wolde he lerne, and gladly teche." William Sievert comments on the pedagogy which went on in the Via Marsala of Rapallo:

[9]*Ibid.*, p. 7.

The "quiet life," however, was frequently disturbed by visits from famous literary and artistic people from all over Europe and, later, by frequent visits from Pound's young followers, for he always was encouraging new talents—he never gave up his role as teacher after he so unceremoniously left Wabash College in Indiana.[10]

Characteristic of his *persona* as preceptor is the text increasingly used by college English classes, *ABC of Reading*, which New Directions made available in paperback in 1960. The subtitle, *Gradus ad Parnassum*, relates it directly to composition: it is principally for the person who desires to ascend as practitioner the mount of the Muses. Moreover, it is for the reader who is receptive, eager to learn, not for those who have arrived at full knowledge of the subject without knowing the facts, as the title page describes pretentiousness in the old. Natural and joyous, Pound's *ABC of Reading* begins in a mood of Mozartian gaiety: "Gloom and solemnity are entirely out of place in even the most rigorous study of an art originally intended to make glad the heart of man."[11] One of the genuinely pivotal books of this century, it lays down a methodology as useful as comparable studies by Eliot.

Taking as a model Pound's own "A Few Don'ts for Imagistes," one might draw up "A Few Do's for Critics" from its pages:

1. Weed out famous but inconsequential writing in order to concentrate on the classics, which never fail to have "a certain and irrepressible freshness."[12]
2. In the spirit of Agassiz, read and compare.
3. Make personal documented statements, in line with the meaning of *criticize* ("to pick out for oneself").[13]
4. Learn to distinguish between "inventors" and "masters."
5. Ground your taste in a thorough knowledge of the best poems, beginning with the oldest in each genre, for example "The Seafarer," where English poetry starts.[14]

The relevance of the last to the composition of Pound's longest work is obvious. Climbing Parnassus requires an apprenticeship in taste to "the singing masters of the soul" who have gone before. Such acquaintance is necessary not only for reasons of technique but also, as *The Cantos*

[10] *The Poetry of Ezra Pound*, p. 9.
[11] *Ibid.*, p. 13.
[12] *Ibid.*, p. 14.
[13] *Ibid.*, p. 30.
[14] *Ibid.*, p. 58.

reveals from its outset, in order to supply material for incorporation into the poetry itself. No one has so well demonstrated as Pound the fragmentary nature of contemporary consciousness. He has gone fishing amidst masterpieces and dumped his glittering catch into the net of his writing, where in the very first Canto (the *Nekuia*) "The Seafarer" jostles the *Odyssey*. To perceive this dependence on the past is to understand what Pound meant by quoting his own discarded lines as headnote to the recent "guidebook" to the *Cantos*: "Say that I dump my catch, shiny and silvery/ As fresh sardines slapping and slipping on the marginal cobbles."[15]

His earlier annotated book list, *How to Read*, Pound judges too polemical to serve in the classroom. However, like the *ABC of Reading*, it is important for its evaluations and definitions. To Allanah Harper he confides that *How to Read* is the outcome of his twenty-five-year struggle to learn something about comparative literature.[16] Fascinating as the volume is, it is in no sense a text.

The second section of the *ABC of Reading* (about a hundred pages) is given over to "exhibits," reaching down in time as far as Whitman in America and Browning in England. Pound accompanies each selection with witty, condensed, casual notes. It is hard to imagine this Baedeker for scholars as having been written so many years ago, so contemporary is its tone. In this last part of the book, passages from the sixteenth-century Mark Alexander Boyd and the seventeenth-century Earl of Dorset resemble the obscurities unearthed by Yvor Winters. Pound calls the citation from Boyd "the most beautiful sonnet in the language";[17] unless one is an expert in Scottish dialect it is difficult to refute him, especially since he may have meant the superlative praise as restricted to works in Boyd's dialect and not to sonnets in the larger tongue, English. Undeniably, the picture of Cupid and his mother, Venus, is lovely, the goddess "a wife ingenuit of the sea/ And lichter nor a dauphin with her fin." Were the comparison to embrace all of English sonnets, Pound's own "A Virginal" has a rather good chance for the distinction which he cavalierly awards to Mark Boyd.

The book ends with a treatise on meter. Those who wish to learn about this topic from Pound go first, quite naturally, to his poetic achievement: hundreds of metrical subtleties abound in each of the *Cantos*. Yet the principles laid down here can help one to profit from his practice. They belong to the "preaching to the mob" which oc-

[15] *Selected Cantos of Ezra Pound*, p. 9.
[16] Rare Book Collection, University of Texas, Austin, Texas.
[17] *ABC of Reading*, p. 34.

cupied the happiest years of his career, a maturity which brought together criticism and poem-making in a fertile interchange. The saying of Saint Francis "We have only so much learning as we put into action" always informs Pound's approach, so that he is never merely theorist.

That the poet conceived of himself as preceptor is clear from that essay of his, in Eliot's culling, entitled "The Teacher's Mission." He envisions this mission as a restoration of language from its corruption through journalism, in order that the "Health of the National Mind" be maintained.[18] No one can achieve success as a teacher unless he first examine his own interior condition—a flashback to Confucius—and then turn toward the light in all openness. In the study of poetry Pound desires, as the furthest possible remove from abstraction, a comparison of masterpieces. This method rests upon disciplined concreteness such as is found in the ideogram's union of word and thing. Administrators should instruct rather than suppress teachers who they feel err. A Franciscan emphasis emanates from sentences like "Education that does not bear on Life and on the most vital and immediate problems of the day is not education but merely suffocation and sabotage."[19]

Accuracy for Pound is a goal consistently held to. In art its corresponding value would be that merit which he believes Jacob Epstein demonstrates in his birds in stone or metal: "They have that greatest quality of art, to wit: certitude."[20] His demolition of "beaneries" through invective in letter, essay, or conversation can be interpreted not as negativism or rancor but rather as a passion for exactness such as one might expect to find in a *Quattrocento* studio or in the laboratory of Louis Agassiz. Whole books like *Jefferson and/or Mussolini* are written in a caustic spirit, to goad readers into making distinctions. At least five *Cantos* enshrine his love for conciseness in their employment of the *ching ming* ideogram, which might well serve as emblem for the intent of all his critical prose.

In addition to the above-mentioned account of metrics which concludes the *ABC of Reading*, some of Pound's best statements on prosody occur in his memoirs of the artist Gaudier-Brzeska, whose notebooks are among his most prized keepsakes. It is here that he speaks of an absolute rhythm as existing for every emotion;[21] of images as having a variable significance, like *a* and *b* and *c* in algebra;[22]

[18] *The Literary Essays of Ezra Pound*, p. 59.
[19] *Ibid*., p. 69.
[20] *The Egoist*, March 16, 1914, p. 108.
[21] *Gaudier-Brzeska*, p. 97.
[22] *Ibid*.

of the image as the poet's pigment,[23] "the word beyond formulated language,"[24] the "radiant node or cluster through which ideas are rushing."[25] In its pages he comments on how colors match certain emotions,[26] reemphasizing his fear of abstractions.[27] In a *dictum* recalling Plato he calls harmony the meeting place of the arts.[28]

Most hostile critics accuse Pound of violating the adage "Shoemaker, stick to your last" because his essays often range far from literature. However, a man lives his life as he chooses: style includes, among other things, the subjects one elects to write about. From at least his forties on, the lion's share of Pound's energies went into economics. It is not extraordinary that an artist whose penury—as did Hart Crane's—forced him to battle to make a living should seize upon money, its nature and distribution as an *idée fixe*. Pound had been brought up on family stories of that pioneer in currency reform, his grandfather Thaddeus C. Pound. Moreover, he was accustomed to visit the glimmering storehouses of silver, gold, and bronze coins at the Philadelphia Mint, where Homer Loomis Pound worked. He early felt the image value of this subject. As an adult, sharp need of money for his dependents as well as for himself caused him to focus more and more on the roots of inequality in a world sufficiently endowed with goods for all men to live a decent life free from painful worry.

In *Vision Fugitive: Ezra Pound and Economics*, Earle Davis has traced the development of Pound's economic theories as these affected his verse and has fitted into their proper place the economists Veblen, Fisher, Douglas, Gesell, del Mar, Kitson, and the others whom Pound unceasingly urged his pupils to absorb. Believing that the Church, which for many centuries had stood firmly for the right use of money, had abandoned its integrity when it permitted usury, he not only stormed and preached but wrote some of the most exquisite poetry of his *Cantos* on this subject: the two on *usura*. Widely depreciated as his theories are, even someone as divergent from him as William Carlos Williams came to accept Pound's position on usury in his epic *Paterson*.

Pound's curriculum is not always to the liking even of those students most sympathetic to him, as Davis notes:

> His voyage, like that of Odysseus, has taken him over strange oceans to hell and back. Some of us have had to row madly to keep him in

[23]*Ibid.*, p. 99
[24]*Ibid.*, p. 102.
[25]*Ibid.*, p. 106.
[26]*Ibid.*, p. 107.
[27]*Ibid.*, p. 136.
[28]*Ibid.*, p. 147.

sight. Some of us wish he had occasionally gone in different directions or had listened to Tiresias. But there he is, the beard sticking out at an angle, the eyes flashing with the light of other worlds, the anchor of Social Credit pulled up safely inside the boat, his rudder set for Ithaca or what he imagines to be paradise.[29]

If one is to comprehend the last fourth of the *Cantos*, he will be forced to learn at least the outline of a history of money, some familiarity with which is needed in order to make any sense of them at all. Realizing how such a requirement will alienate readers, Pound nevertheless thinks the issue important enough to take that risk.

From those days in Venice, when he lived largely on barley soup in the *trattorie* of San Gregorio, to the Rome or Rapallo diatribes against monetary abuses as the source of wars and other public evils, Pound advanced from an experiential student of poverty into the professor's chair. He never forgot his "laboratory" realization of what it meant to be poor. Unable to agree with men who, like Arthur Griffiths, failed to see economics as a force capable of eliciting an emotional as well as an intellectual reaction, he gave his voice, as well as pen, pencil, or typewriter, both on the Italian Riviera and during those last incarcerated years in America, to educating those who would listen or read.

Pound has ever been quick to commend those few academic preceptors whom he regards as outstanding. At Saint Elizabeth's in the 1950s, he wrote with warm remembrance to a favorite elementary-school instructor, Florence Ridpath, by that time retired to a Methodist home in Philadelphia. He describes her to Carl Gatter: "She was a teacher the kids liked, and that, I suppose, ran counter to the efficiency mania for crushing humanity out of existence."[30] From Italy earlier he had written an expression of condolence to Professor Roy F. Nichols and the rest of the University of Pennsylvania history department when a colleague of theirs died suddenly:

> The idea that a student might have a legitimate curiosity was in no way alien to his [Dr. Ames's] sensibilities. All of which goes into the making of a strong personal affection lasting over three decades with no more nutriment than perhaps two or three letters.[31]

That very February Pound had sent Professor Ames a letter, though it arrived after the death. *The Cantos*, as well as correspondence, testifies that Doolittle, Shepard, Schelling, Rennert were not forgotten by their

[29] *Vision Fugitive: Ezra Pound and Economics*, p. 202.
[30] Rare Book and Manuscript Collection, Free Library of Philadelphia.
[31] Rare Book Collection, University of Texas, Austin, Texas.

pupil. Yet though he could praise, he could be scathing where he saw mediocrity, a failure of imagination, or pomposity.

Originally, it had been Pound's intention to devote his own life to teaching, and, as William Sievert affirms, in a broad sense he has done so:

> By this time [1908], he had earned his Master of Arts degree from the University; he was ready to begin a career which in one way or another he would continue for the rest of his life; the career was that of teacher.[32]

Eliot, writing in *The Literary Essays of Ezra Pound*, says: "He has always been first and foremost, a teacher and campaigner."[33] Dedicated to Basil Bunting and Louis Zukofsky, *Guide to Kulchur* shows him in this light. It is based upon the theme which Clark Emery used for the title of his volume on Pound, *Ideas into Action*. In Emery's words, "The history of a culture is the history of ideas going into action."[34] If Pound infuriates with his rock-drill persistence, he does so designedly. Having no personal interest to advance, but merely the cause of truth as he sees it, he romps about in iconoclastic glee easily mistaken for temper. He is serious in the manner that Molière and Jonson are serious. Under his sometimes heavy-handed wit runs the desire for betterment which he believes should animate the critic, who is no idle smeller of roses but a fierce enemy of stupidity and ignorance, close companions though not identical twins. Both criticism and poetry to Pound are didactic, an epithet he would acknowledge as unashamedly as Dante. Education he has called the art of making distinctions, an art in which Pound excels whether in prose or in poetry. One example is his gift for definition, as in: "Art is a fluid moving above or over the minds of men."[35] In *The Spirit of Romance* he says quite frankly: "The aim of the present work is to instruct. Its ambition is to instruct painlessly."[36] His essays do just that, whereas the instruction effected by his verse, since its wisdom is harder to "earn," may not always be painless.

In such prose works as *Guide to Kulchur*, Pound reveals the breadth of his reading, just as the canon of his works reveals the scope of his tremendous creative talents. Where among today's writers can we find one who has investigated more thoroughly Stevenson's "The world is so full of a number of things"? He is indeed a reconstruction of the Renais-

---

[32] *The Poetry of Ezra Pound*, p. 7.
[33] *Ibid.*, p. xii.
[34] *Ibid.*, p. 44.
[35] *The Spirit of Romance*, p. 7.
[36] *Ibid.*, p. 8.

sance "complete man" (*polumetis*). Like Mauberley, he seems to have been born out of his age—to be, in fact, a composite of several ages. Music, painting, sculpture, as well as literature, fall under his scrutiny. The *Quattrocento* would have been a natural milieu for him: "The fifteenth century is, above all, that of the many-sided man. There is no biography that does not, besides the chief work of its hero, speak of other pursuits, all of which pass beyond mere dilettantism."[37] Lyrics, letters, plays, translations, operas—in all he excels, just as he is at home in every century and on every continent.

Pound's latest critical thought lies in his notes to *Confucius to Cummings: An Anthology of Poetry*, compiled with Marcella Spann, now a young English teacher in a Connecticut college and in a position to carry out her preceptor's theories as well as to promulgate his preferences in literature. Containing almost a hundred selections, the book is meant for the reader who knows only English. It might be considered a second-semester text, to follow the *ABC of Reading*. As indicated in the title, the anthology commences with the sixth-century B.C. Chinese sage, out of whose writings Pound picks a poem called "Confucius," which he annotates with the words "Here the actual author speaks."[38] Out of line with the stance on voice and address of the influential *Understanding Poetry*, edited by Cleanth Brooks and Robert Penn Warren, he qualifies by stating that "I" and the poet are one, since after all the piece is a dramatic monologue: the same fusion, contrary to the thesis of this text, holds true again and again in autobiographical sequences of the *Cantos*, though recognition of this identity is slow in coming.

All Pound scholars approach this book with curiosity about its inclusions from among the entire spectrum of world literature. Homer, of course, they expect to find present, and he is. Among all the available translations, it is to George Chapman that Pound turns here for a poetic rendition, possibly because, except for Alexander Pope, he was the greatest writer (outside of Pound himself) to attempt the translation of the *Odyssey*. If his choice among versions of Aeschylus is puzzling, it may be that he settled on Dallas Simpson's Negro-dialect opening of the *Agamemnon* to serve as a spoof on those who take their classics too solemnly, a danger pointed out in the *ABC of Reading*. In the medieval section, there appears Pound's own translation of Saint Francis's "Cantico del Sole,"[39] little known although it is probably the very best version to date.

In the third Appendix, Pound sets down three questions that any

---

[37]Jacob Burckhardt, *The Civilization of the Renaissance in Italy and Other Selections*, ed. Alexander Dru, p. 233.
[38]*Confucius to Cummings: An Anthology of Poetry*, p. 8.
[39]*Ibid.*, pp. 86-88.

teacher using this text should first ask himself and then propose to his students:

(a) Why is the poem included in the anthology?
(b) What moved the author to write it?
(c) What does it tell the reader?[40]

These three points are crucial in that they constitute an approach based on affirmative reactions, always far more productive of helpful criticism than fault-finding, as Pound implies in paraphrasing his former English teacher Felix Schelling.[41] In this collection he remarks, as he has elsewhere, that only from the artist will notable criticism come.[42] Hardly an incontrovertible view, it is nevertheless his position, and he maintains it.

Within the texture of Pound's chef d'oeuvre, critical insights of his own or in reported talk appear from time to time as evidences of the civilized man's concern about language. In Canto 80 he writes: "To communicate and then stop, that is the law of discourse," rephrasing the adage in Canto 87 as "Get the meaning across and then quit." These sentences go far toward explaining his silence of recent years, so bewildering to those used to his ebullient youth and middle age. The ideogram *chih*, "to stop or desist," occurs in Canto 52 for the first time, bearing the same significance as these two maxims above; Canto 60 expands it:

> He ordered 'em to prepare a total anatomy, et
> qu'ils veillèrent à la pureté du langage
> qu'on n'employât que de termes propres
> (namely CH'ing ming)

A half-dozen Cantos incorporate this ideogram, even as late as Canto 110, wherein Pound uses it twice. In Canto 77 it takes the form of "the precise definition," a crystallization of his Imagist tenet, in fact the height toward which the *Cantos* in their rising sweep endlessly strive.

Though *The Cantos* is the essential Pound, his prose works soar far above journalism and have had enormous impact in promoting the enjoyment of a myriad of heretofore unknown literary personages, besides directing the talents of his younger contemporaries. Not only are they pleasurable reading for their own sake but they are indispensable for the light they throw on the poetry.

[40]*Ibid.*, p. 335.
[41]*Ibid.*, p. 322.
[42]*Ibid.*, p. 340.

T. S. Eliot

Introduction to Selected Poems of Ezra Pound

Mr. Ezra Pound recently made for publication in New York a volume of "collected poems" under the title of *Personae.*[1] I made a few suggestions for omissions and inclusions in a similar collection to be published in London; and out of discussions of such matters with Pound arose the specter of an introduction by myself.

The poems which I wished to include, from among those which the author had omitted, are found together at the back of the book. The order followed throughout the book is, with the exception mentioned, that of original publication of the scattered volumes from which the poems are drawn.

Mr. Pound intended his collection to consist of all of his work in verse up to his *Cantos,* which he chooses to keep in print. This book, so far as I am responsible for it, is not intended for quite that role: it is not a "collected edition" but a selection. Some of the poems omitted by Pound, as well as some of those omitted by myself, seem to me well "worthy of preservation." This book is, in my eyes, rather a convenient Introduction to Pound's work than a definitive edition. The volumes previously published represent each a particular aspect or period of his

---

[1] That title could not be given to the present book, because it would lead to confusion with the American volume, and with the original *Personae* published in 1909 by Elkin Mathews.

Introduction to Selected Poems of Ezra Pound, *ed. T. S. Eliot (London: Faber & Gwyer, Ltd., 1928). Reprinted by permission of Faber & Faber, Ltd.*

work; and even when they fall into the right hands, are not always read in the right order. My point is that Pound's work is not only much more varied than is generally supposed, but also represents a continuous development, down to *Hugh Selwyn Mauberley,* the last stage of importance before the *Cantos.* This book would be, were it nothing else, a text-book of modern versification. The *Cantos* "of a poem of some length" are by far his most important achievement; owing to their scarcity and their difficulty, they are not appreciated; but they are much more comprehensible to a reader who has followed the author's poetry from the beginning.

I remarked some years ago, in speaking of *vers libre,* that "no *vers* is *libre* for the man who wants to do a good job." The term, which fifty years ago had an exact meaning, in relation to the French alexandrine, now means too much to mean anything at all. The *vers libre* of Jules Laforgue, who, if not quite the greatest French poet after Baudelaire, was certainly the most important technical innovator, is free verse in much the way that the later verse of Shakespeare, Webster, Tourneur, is free verse: that is to say, it stretches, contracts, and distorts the traditional French measure as later Elizabethan and Jacobean poetry stretches, contracts and distorts the blank verse measure. But the term is applied to several types of verse which have developed in English without relation to Laforgue, Corbière, and Rimbaud, or to each other. To be more precise, there are, for instance, my own type of verse, that of Pound, and that of the disciples of Whitman. I will not say that subsequently there have not appeared traces of reciprocal influence of several types upon one another, but I am here speaking of origins. My own verse is, so far as I can judge, nearer to the original meaning of *vers libre* than is any of the other types: at least, the form in which I began to write, in 1908 or 1909, was directly drawn from the study of Laforgue together with the later Elizabethan drama; and I do not know anyone who started from exactly that point. I did not read Whitman until much later in life, and had to conquer an aversion to his form, as well as to much of his matter, in order to do so. I am equally certain—it is indeed obvious— that Pound owes nothing to Whitman. This is an elementary observation; but when dealing with popular conceptions of *vers libre* one must still be as simple and elementary as fifteen years ago.

The earliest of the poems in the present volume show that the first strong influences upon Pound, at the moment when his verse was taking direction, were those of Browning and Yeats. In the background are the 'Nineties in general, and behind the 'Nineties, of course, Swinburne and William Morris. I suspect that the latter influences were much more visible in whatever Mr. Pound wrote before the first of his published verse; they linger in some of his later work more as an emotional attitude than in the technique of versification: the shades of Dowson, Lionel Johnson and Fiona flit about.[2] Technically, these influences were all good; for they combine to insist upon the importance of *verse as speech* (I am not excepting Swinburne); while from more anti-quarian studies Pound was learning the importance of *verse as song.*

It is important at the point to draw a simple distinction which is overlooked by nearly all critics who are not verse-makers themselves, and by many who are: the distinction between form and substance, and again between material and attitude. Such distinctions are constantly drawn, but are often drawn when they should not be, as well as ignored when they should be observed. Modern verse is often associated where it is different, and distinguished where it is the same. People may think they like the form because they like the content, or think they like the content because they like the form. In the perfect poet they fit and are the same thing; and in another sense they *always* are the same thing. So it is always true to say that form and content are the same thing, and always true to say that they are different things.

Pound, for example, has been accused of exactly opposite faults, because these distinctions are seldom observed in the right place. He is called objectionably "modern," and objectionably "antiquarian." Neither is true at the point at which it is supposed to be true.

I should say first that Pound's versification is objectionable to those who object to it as "modern," because they have not sufficient education (in verse) to understand development. Poets may be divided into those who develop technique, those who imitate technique, and those who invent technique. When I say "invent," I should use inverted commas, for invention would be irreproachable if it were possible. "Invention" is wrong only because it is impossible. I mean that the difference between the "development" and the "sport" is, in poetry, a capital one. There are two kinds of "sports" in poetry, in the floricultural sense. One is the imitation of development, and the other is the imitation of some Idea of originality. The former is common-place, a waste product of civilization. The latter is contrary to life. The poem which is absolutely original is absolutely bad; it is, in the bad sense, "subjective" with no relation to the world to which it appeals.

[2] Mr. Pound, it must be remembered, has written an excellent brief study of the verse of Arthur Symons, and has edited a volume of the poems of Lionel Johnson, some few copies of which contained an introduction by the editor, hastily withdrawn from circulation by the publisher and now a bibliophile's rarity.

Originality, in other words, is by no means a simple idea in the criticism of poetry. True originality is merely development; and if it is right development it may appear in the end so *inevitable* that we almost come to the point of view of denying all "original" virtue to the poet. He simply did the next thing. I do not deny that *true* and *spurious* originality may hit the public with the same shock; indeed spurious originality ("spurious" when we use the word "originality" properly, that is to say, within the limitations of life, and when we use the word absolutely and therefore improperly, "genuine") may give the greater shock.

Now Pound's originality is genuine in that his versification is a *logical* development of the verse of his English predecessors. Whitman's originality is both genuine and spurious. It is genuine in so far as it is a *logical* development of certain English prose; Whitman was a great prose writer. It is spurious in so far as Whitman wrote in a way that asserted that his great prose was a new form of verse. (And I am ignoring in this connection the large part of clap-trap in Whitman's content.) The word "revolutionary" has no meaning, for this reason: we confound under the same name those who are revolutionary because they develop logically, and those who are "revolutionary" because they innovate illogically. It is *very* difficult, at any moment, to discriminate between the two.

Pound is "original," in the way which I approve, in another sense. There is a shallow test which holds that the original poet goes direct to life, and the derivative poet to "literature." When we look into the matter, we find that the poet who is really "derivative" is the poet who *mistakes* literature for life, and very often the reason why he makes this mistake is that—he has not read enough. The ordinary life of ordinary cultivated people is a mush of literature and life. There is a right sense in which for the educated person literature *is* life, and life *is* literature; and there is also a vicious sense in which the same phrases may be true. We can at least try not to confuse the material and the use which the author makes of it.

Now Pound is often most "original" in the right sense, when he is most "archaeological" in the ordinary sense. It is almost too platitudinous to say that one is not modern by writing about chimney-pots, or archaic by writing about oriflammes. It is true that most people who write of oriflammes are merely collecting old coins, as most people who write about chimney-pots are merely forging new ones. If one can really penetrate the life of another age, one is penetrating the life of one's own. The poet who understands merlons and crenelles can understand chimney-pots, and vice versa. Some men can understand the architecture of the cathedral of Albi, for instance, by seeing it as a biscuit factory; others can understand a biscuit factory best by thinking of the cathedral of Albi. It is merely a subjective difference of method. The mole digs and the eagle flies, but their end is the same, to exist.

One of Pound's most indubitable claims to genuine originality is, I believe, his revivification of the Provençal and the early Italian poetry. The people who tire of Pound's Provence and Pound's Italy are those who cannot see Provence and medieval Italy except as museum pieces, which is not how Pound sees them, or how he makes others see them. It is true that Pound seems to me to see Italy through Provence, where I see Provence through Italy (the fact that I am totally ignorant of Provençal, except for a dozen lines of Dante, has nothing to do with the matter). But he does see them as contemporary with himself, that is to say, he has grasped certain things in Provence and Italy which are permanent in human nature. He is much more modern, in my opinion, when he deals with Italy and Provence, than when he deals with modern life. His Bertrand de Born is much more living than his Mr. Hecatomb Styrax *(Moeurs Contemporains).* When he deals with antiquities, he extracts the essentially living; when he deals with contemporaries, he sometimes notes only the accidental. But this does not mean that he is antiquarian or parasitical on literature. Any scholar can see Arnaut Daniel or Guido Cavalcanti as literary figures; only Pound can see them as living beings. Time, in such connections, does not matter; it is irrelevant whether what you see, really see, as a human being, is Arnaut Daniel or your greengrocer. It is merely a question of the means suited to the particular poet, and we are more concerned with the end than with the means.

In Pound's earlier poems then, we must take account first of the influence of certain predecessors in English poetry, and second of the influence of Provençal and Italian. In each of these influences we must distinguish between influence of form and influence of content; but, on the other hand, no one can be influenced by form or by content without being influenced by the other; and the tangle of influences is one which we can only partially resolve. Any particular influence of one poet on another is both of form and content. The former is perhaps the easier to trace. Certain of the early poems are obviously affected by the technical influence of Yeats. It is easier to trace the influence of the exact and difficult Provençal versification, than to distinguish the element of genuine revivification of Provençal, from the element of romantic fantasy which Pound acquired, not from Arnaut Daniel or Dante, but from the 'Nineties. But it must be remembered that these things are different, whether we are competent to perform the analysis or not.

There is a definite advance in *Ripostes* of 1912 beyond *Personae* of 1910. Some indications of the point of view of this period are found in notes reprinted in a prose book, *Pavannes and Divisions* (Knopf, 1918), entitled "Retrospect," and a note on "Dolmetsch and Vers Libre." Probably the most important poem in this group is the version of the Anglo-Saxon "Seafarer." It is a new assimilation, subsequent to the Provençal, and with that a preparation for the paraphrases from the Chinese, *Cathay*; which in turn is a necessary stage in the progress towards the *Cantos*, which are wholly himself. Throughout the work of Pound there is what we might call a steady effort towards the synthetic construction of a style of speech. In each of the elements or strands there is something of Pound and something of some other, not further analyzable; the strands go to make one rope, but the rope is not yet complete. And good translation like this is not merely translation, for the translator is giving the original through himself, and finding himself through the original. And again, in following the work of Pound, we must remember two aspects: there is the aspect of versification, traced through his early influences, through his work on Provençal, Italian and Anglo-Saxon, on the Chinese poets and on Propertius; and there is the aspect of deeper personal feeling, which is not invariably, so far, found in the poems of most important technical accomplishment. The two things tend in course of time to unite; but in the poems under consideration they often are distinct, sometimes imperfectly united. Hence those who are moved most by technical accomplishment see a steady progress; those who care most for the personal voice are apt to think that Pound's early verse is the best. Neither are quite right; but the second are the more wrong. *Ripostes* is, I think, a more personal volume than the earlier *Personae* and *Exultations*; some poems in *Lustra* continue this development and some do not; *Cathay* and *Propertius* are more directly important on the technical side, as is *The Seafarer;* it is not until we reach *Mauberley* (much the finest poem, I believe, before the *Cantos*) that some definite fusion takes place. The reader should compare some of the lovely small poems in *Ripostes* with the poems in *Canzoni, Personae*, and *Exultations* which are of more manifest technical interest, and on the other hand with *Mauberley*. Meanwhile, in *Lustra* are many voices. In the beautiful "Near Perigord" in *Lustra* there is the voice of Browning. There is also

There shut up in his castle, Tairiran's,
She who had nor ears nor tongue save in her hands,

Gone—ah, gone—untouched, unreachable!
She who could never live save through one person,
She who could never speak save to one person,
And all the rest of her a shifting change,
A broken bundle of mirrors. . . .

These verses are not Browning, or anybody else but Pound; but they
are not the final Pound either; for there is too much in the phrasing
that might have been constructed by a various number of good poets.
It is fine poetry; it is more "personal" than *Cathay;* but the syntax is
less significant. In *Ripostes* and in *Lustra* there are many short poems
of a slighter build than this, equally moving, but in which also the
"feeling" or "mood" is more interesting than the writing. (In the perfect poem both are equally interesting, and being equally interesting
are interesting as one thing and not as two.)

A GIRL

The tree has entered my hands,
The sap has ascended my arms,
The tree has grown into my breast—
Downward,
The branches grow out of me, like arms.

Tree you are,
Moss you are,
You are violets with wind above them.
A child—*so* high—you are,
And all this is folly to the world.

There, you see, the "feeling" is original in the best sense, but the
phrasing is not quite "completed"; for the last line is one which I or
half a dozen other men might have written. Yet it is not "wrong," and
I certainly could not improve upon it.

As for *Cathay,* it must be pointed out that Pound is the inventor of
Chinese poetry for our time. I suspect that every age has had, and will
have, the same illusion concerning translations, an illusion which
is not altogether an illusion either. When a foreign poet is successfully done into the idiom of our own language and our own
time, we believe that he has been "translated"; we believe that
through this translation we really at last get the original. The
Elizabethans must have thought that they *got* Homer through
Chapman, Plutarch through North. Not being Elizabethans, we have
not that illusion; we see that Chapman is more Chapman than Homer,

and North more North than Plutarch, both localized three hundred years ago. We perceive also that modern scholarly translations, Loeb or other, do not give us what the Tudors gave. If a modern Chapman, or North or Florio appeared, we should believe that he was the real translator; we should, in other words, do him the compliment of believing that his translation was translucence. For contemporaries, no doubt the Tudor translations were translucencies; for us they are "magnificent specimens of Tudor prose." The same fate impends upon Pound. His translations seem to be—and that is the test of excellence—translucencies: we *think* we are closer to the Chinese than when we read, for instance, Legge. I doubt this: I predict that in three hundred years Pound's *Cathay* will be a "Windsor Translation" as Chapman and North are now "Tudor Translations": it will be called (and justly) a "magnificent specimen of XXth Century poetry" rather than a "translation." Each generation must translate for itself.

This is as much as to say that Chinese poetry, as we know it today, is something invented by Ezra Pound. It is not to say that there is a Chinese poetry-in-itself, waiting for some ideal translator who shall be only translator; but that Pound has enriched modern English poetry as Fitzgerald enriched it. But whereas Fitzgerald produced only the one great poem, Pound's translation is interesting also because it is a phase in the development of Pound's poetry. People of today who like Chinese poetry are really no more liking Chinese poetry than the people who like Willow pottery and Chinesische-Turms in Munich and Kew like Chinese Art. It is probable that the Chinese, as well as the Provençals and the Italians and the Saxons, influenced Pound, for no one can work intelligently with a foreign matter without being affected by it; on the other hand, it is certain that Pound has influenced the Chinese and the Provençals and the Italians and the Saxons—not the matter *an sich*, which is unknowable, but the matter as we know it.

To consider Pound's original work and his translation separately would be a mistake, a mistake which implies a greater mistake about the nature of translation. (Cf. his "Notes on Elizabethan Classicists" in *Pavannes and Divisions,* pp. 186 ff.) If Pound had not been a translator, his reputation as an "original" poet would be higher; if he had not been an original poet, his reputation as a "translator" would be higher; and this is all irrelevant.

Those who expect that any good poet should proceed by turning out a series of masterpieces, each similar to the last, only more developed *in every way,* are simply ignorant of the conditions under which the poet must work, especially in our time. The poet's progress is dual. There is the gradual accumulation of experience, like a tantalus jar: it may be only once in five or ten years that experience accumulates to form a new whole and finds its appropriate expression. But if a poet were content to attempt nothing less than always his best, if he insisted on waiting for these unpredictable crystallizations, he would not be ready for them when they came. The development of experience is largely unconscious, subterranean, so that we cannot gauge its progress except once in every five to ten years; but in the meantime the poet must be working; he must be experimenting and trying his technique so that it will be ready, like a well-oiled fire-engine, when the moment comes to strain it to its utmost. The poet who wishes to continue to write poetry must keep in training; and must do this, not by forcing his inspiration, but by good workmanship on a level possible for some hours' work every week of his life.

What I have just said should serve as an introduction, not only to the translations, but to a class of Pound's poems which may be called the Epigrams. These occur *passim* throughout *Lustra.* I have included most of them in this edition. There is, of course, acquaintance with Martial as well as with the epigrammatists of the Greek Anthology. Among "poetry lovers" of the present time a taste for Martial is still more rare than a (genuine) taste for Dryden; what "poetry lovers" do not recognize is that their limitation of poetry to the "poetical" is a modern restriction of the romantic age: the romantic age has decided that a great deal of prose is poetry (though I dare say that Burton, and Browne, and De Quincey, and other idols of the poetry-prose romanticists presumed that they were writing prose); and conversely that a good deal of poetry is prose. (To me, Pope is poetry and Jeremy Taylor is prose.) The reader must not be hasty in deciding whether Pound's epigrams "come off"; for he should first examine his own soul to find out whether he is capable of enjoying the very best epigram as poetry. (Mackail's selections from the Greek Anthology are admirable except for being selections: that is, they tend to suppress the element of wit, the element of epigram, in the anthologists.) The reader who does not like Pound's epigrams should make very sure that he is not comparing them with the *Ode to a Nightingale* before he condemns them. He would do best to try to accept them as a peculiar genre, and compare them with each other—for some are indeed better than others, and I have even omitted one on Mr. Chesterton—before he compares them with anything else. No one is competent to judge poetry until he recognizes that poetry is nearer to "verse" than it is to prose poetry.

I am not prepared to say that I appreciate epigrams: my taste is possibly too romantic. All that I am sure of is that Pound's epigrams, if compared with anything contemporary of similar genre, are definitely better. And I am sure also of this, that Pound's occupation with translations and paraphrases, and with the lighter forms of serious verse, provide evidence of the integrity of his purpose. One cannot write poetry all the time; and when one cannot write poetry, it is better to write what one knows is verse and make it good verse, than to write bad verse and persuade oneself that it is good poetry. Pound's epigrams and translations represent a rebellion against the romantic tradition which insists that a poet should be continuously inspired, which allows the poet to present bad verse as poetry, but denies him the right to make good verse unless it can also pass as great poetry.

This introduction will serve its purpose if it makes clear to the reader one point: that a poet's work may proceed along two lines on an imaginary graph; one of the lines being his conscious and continuous effort in technical excellence, that is, in continually developing his medium for the moment when he really has something to say. The other line is just his normal human course of development, his accumulation and digestion of experience (experience is not sought for, it is merely accepted in consequence of doing what we really want to do), and by experience I mean the results of reading and reflection, varied interests of all sorts, contacts and acquaintances, as well as passion and adventure. Now and then the two lines may converge at a high peak, so that we get a masterpiece. That is to say, an accumulation of experience has crystallized to form material or art, and years of work in technique have prepared an adequate medium; and something results in which medium and material, form and content, are indistinguishable. A semi-metaphorical account like this must not be applied too literally; even if it could be applied to the work of all poets, the work of each individual poet would exhibit some deviation from it; I posit it only as an introduction to the work of *some* poets, of whom Pound is one. It should help us to analyse his work, to distinguish his work of the first, second and third degree of intensity, and to appreciate the value of the lower degrees.

At this point the objection may be raised: even if the account of the process is correct, is it justifiable for a poet to publish any of his work but that in which perfection of form unites with significance of feeling; any, that is, but his very best? There are several rejoinders to this objection, both theoretical and practical: one of the simplest being that if you apply it you must apply it both ways, and the result would be to censor a larger part of the published work of most of the accepted poets. It might also expunge several excellent poets altogether. I have met but very few people in my life who really care for poetry; and those few, when they have the knowledge (for they are

sometimes quite illiterate people), know how to take from every poet
what he has to give, and reject only those poets who whatever they
give always pretend to give *more* than they do give; these discerning
people appreciate the work of Pope and Dryden (indeed it might be
said in our time that the man who cannot enjoy Pope as poetry
probably understands no poetry: incidentally, I remember that Pound
once induced me to destroy what I thought an excellent set of
couplets; for, said he, "Pope has done this so well that you cannot do
it better; and if you mean this as a burlesque, you had better suppress
it, for you cannot parody Pope unless you can write better verse than
Pope—and you can't"). I have just described the relation of a poet's
technical development and his personal development as two curves on a
graph which sometimes meet. But I should add that the metaphor is
deceptive if it makes you suppose that the two things are quite distinct.
If we only knew "perfect" poetry we should know very little about
poetry; we cannot say even who are the twelve, or the six, or the three,
or the two "greatest" poets. But if we really love poetry, then we know
and must know all its degrees. The distinction between technique and
feeling—a distinction necessarily arbitrary and brutal—will not bother
us: we shall be able to appreciate what is good of its kind; we shall be
able to appreciate the meeting of the peaks, the fusion of matter and
means, form and content, on any level; and also we shall appreciate
both poetry in which technical excellence surpasses interest of content,
and poetry in which interest of content surpasses technique.

In this volume you will find poetry of all three kinds. In some of
the verse I believe that the content is more important than the means
of expression; in others the means of expression is the important thing;
some combines both. Most people will find things that they like in this
book, and things that they dislike; only persons who like poetry and
have trained themselves to like poetry will like it all. And of such
persons there are not many.

The closest approximation—I mean the most nearly continuous
identification—of form and feeling in Pound's poetry, I find in his
Cantos, of which I can say but little, as I am not permitted to print
them in this book. (At least, they are the only "poem of some length"
by any of my contemporaries that I can read with enjoyment and
admiration; at most, they are more than I could deal with anyway in
this essay; in any case, they are a mine for juvenile poets to quarry; and
in any case, my disagreement with their "philosophy" is another
affair.) But concerning the contents of this book, I am quite certain of
Mauberley, whatever else I am certain of. I have omitted one long
poem, which Mr. Pound might himself have included: the *Homage to*

Sextus Propertius. I was doubtful of its effect upon the uninstructed reader, even with my instructions. If the uninstructed reader is not a classical scholar, he will make nothing of it; if he be a classical scholar, he will wonder why this does not conform to his notions of what translation should be. It is not a translation, it is a paraphrase, or still more truly (for the instructed) a *persona.* It is also a criticism of Propertius, a criticism which in a most interesting way insists upon an element of humour, of irony and mockery, in Propertius, which Mackail and other interpreters have missed. I think that Pound is critically right, and that Propertius was more civilized than most of his interpreters have admitted; nevertheless, I have thought best to omit the poem—though it is a most interesting study in versification, and one of the necessary prolegomena to the *Cantos.* I felt that the poem, *Homage to Propertius,* would give difficulty to many readers: because it is not enough a "translation," and because it is, on the other hand, too much a "translation," to be intelligible to any but the accomplished student of Pound's poetry.[3]

It may give surprise that I attach so much importance to *Hugh Selwyn Mauberley.* This seems to me a great poem. On the one hand, I perceive that the versification is more accomplished than that of any other of the poems in this book, and more varied. I only pretend to know as much about versifying as my carpenter knows about woodwork, or my painter knows about distemper. But I know very well that the apparent roughness and *naïveté* of the verse and rhyming of *Mauberley* are inevitably the result of many years of hard work: if you cannot appreciate the dexterity of *Altaforte* you cannot appreciate the simplicity of *Mauberley.* On the other side, the poem seems to me, when you have marked the sophistication and the great variety of the verse, verse of a man who knows his way about, to be a positive document of sensibility. It is compact of the experience of a certain man in a certain place at a certain time; and it is also a document of an epoch; it is genuine tragedy and comedy; and it is, in the best sense of Arnold's worn phrase, a "criticism of life."

I wish that it were suitable and permissible for me to proceed to discuss the *Cantos,* and Pound's philosophy. But in any case it is not desirable for me to expound these matters except with those who accept his poetry as I accept it.

---

[3] It is, in my opinion, a better criticism of Propertius than M. Benda's *Properce.* I observe in passing that it was Mr. Pound who introduced Benda to England and America.

Part III

Specific Works and Stages

Thomas H. Jackson

Research and the Uses of London

> *To write on [his] plan, it was at least necessary*
> *to read and think. No man could be born a . . .*
> *poet, nor assume the dignity of a writer, by*
> *descriptions copied from descriptions, by imi-*
> *tations borrowed from imitations, by traditional*
> *imagery, and hereditary similes, by readiness of*
> *rhyme, and volubility of syllables.* —Samuel
> Johnson, "Life of Cowley"

A Lume Spento, for the most part containing poems Pound had
written before he went to Europe, was published privately in Venice in
1908. Shortly after arriving in London, he had *Quinzaine for This Yule*
printed.[1] *Personae* came out in the spring of 1909 and *Exultations* in
the fall of the same year. At the time Exultations went to press, Pound
was working on the third chapter of *The Spirit of Romance*, and in
1910 Small, Maynard, and Company published his *Provença*, a selection

[1] YL 115 (September 9, 1909) to Homer L. Pound.

From "Research and the Uses of London," in The Early Poetry of Ezra
Pound, *by Thomas H. Jackson (Cambridge, Mass.: Harvard University
Press, 1969), pp. 189–97. Reprinted by permission of the publishers.
Copyright 1968 by the President and Fellows of Harvard College:
Copyright 1968 by Ezra Pound: all previously uncollected or unpub-
lished material, including letters. Reprinted by permission of New Di-
rections Publishing Corporation, Agents for the Estate of Ezra Pound.*

from the earlier poems plus a few that were to appear in *Canzoni* the next year. Such a rapid succession of books should make us cautious about an over-ready use of the term "development," but the collections published after *A Lume Spento* reveal changes that look ahead to the features of Pound's more mature work.

From a biographical point of view, it is evident that London made a strong impression on him. We can see some sort of dawn breaking in a 1909 letter to his father in which Pound says that Elkin Mathews, the Vigo Street publisher, "has turned his shelves over to me to browse in and I find the contemporary people seem to be making as good stuff as the theoretical giants of the past" (*YL* 99). A few weeks after Mathews published *Personae*, Pound wrote to William Carlos Williams that "There is no town like London to make one feel the vanity of all art except the highest. To make one disbelieve in all but the most careful conservative presentation of one's stuff." "I have," he adds, "printed too much" (*L* 8). The contents of *Personae* imply that, development aside for the moment, some accession of self-criticism had taken place. Along with seventeen previously unpublished poems, it reproduces only sixteen from *A Lume Spento*—which might mean little except that this abandonment of the other twenty-nine poems represents in most cases a permanent excision. Four of the twenty-nine reappeared in *Exultations*— "Plotinus," "The Eyes," "On His Own Face in a Glass," and "To the Dawn: Defiance"—but, even so, over half of the original collection was consigned to the comparative obscurity of collections of rare books. The process of excision continued: though *Provença* is described on its title page as "Poems Selected from *Personae, Exultations,* and *Canzoniere*," the selection represents a permanent garnering, and we find the group from *A Lume Spento* already largely stabilized; only "Camaraderie," "Ballad for Gloom," and "In Tempore Senectutis" remain to be excised to make what constitutes its current published remains. Nevertheless, nearly half of the *Personae* of 1909 consists of poems from the first collection, a fact suggesting the essential continuity of all three books, both technical and thematic.

But granted that we are to be chary of claiming to see development in books published not much more than a year apart, *Personae* and *Exultations* are exploratory in a way different from *A Lume Spento*. Certainly the two later collections were as tentative as the first: of the thirty-four new poems, only ten appear in the current edition of *Personae*, which means that they have fared slightly worse than *A Lume Spento* with its fourteen survivals from an original forty-five. Many of the poems from *Personae* and *Exultations* were omitted even from *Provença* a year later, and in *Umbra*, Pound's presentation in 1920 of "all that he now wishes to keep in circulation" from the earlier collections, the number of survivals is already down to sixteen. But this is simply editorial information; the poems themselves are ample evidence of what Pound was doing. Although even in *A Lume Spento* Pound experimented with "rules of Spanish, Anglo-Saxon and Greek metric" (*L* 4), that first collection, compared to *Personae* and *Exultations,* was primarily an interim report—a calling card for his London appearance. Its exploratory quality makes it seem a beginning poet's attempt to find out what he can do, whereas the following three or four seek rather to find out what can be done. It is as if his confrontation by "the contemporary people," some of whom showed "what the people of second rank can do, and what damned good work it is" (*L* 8), had suddenly made him aware of how unsatisfactory his own first fruits were; for if *A Lume Spento* betrays ties of a certain kind with the nineteenth century, *Personae* and especially *Exultations* already show signs of a vigorous attempt to expand the expressive limits set by those ties.

The attempt accounts for one of the more curious differences between the first collection and at least the following two: not a lessening of perceptible "influences," as we might expect, but an intensification of them. Many of the poems in *Personae* and *Exultations* are not profitably describable except in terms of influence—and this for the simple reason that, confronted (presumably) by evidence of his limitations, of the sheltered nature of his experience of living poetry, Pound begins deliberately to expand his knowledge and his practical command of the poetically possible. For example, the attraction of Yeats and "Celticism" for Pound seems to have grown almost as much from their conducing to interesting visual possibilities as from their offering new modes of experience—although the two considerations are so closely related that even to call them considerations amounts to hedging. At any rate, experiments in this vein form part of both *Personae* and *Exultations.*

There is, to begin with, "Nils Lykke" in *Exultations*:

> Beautiful, infinite memories
> That are a-plucking at my heart,
> Why will you be ever calling and a-calling,
> And a-murmuring in the dark there?
>
> And a-reaching out your long hands
> Between me and my beloved?

The obviously Yeatsian rhythms in this poem and its Yeatsian "sentiments" remind us of Pound's remark that "It is only good manners if

you repeat a few other men to at least do it better or more briefly"
(*L* 6). If "Nils Lykke" is not better than "He Remembers Forgotten
Beauty," it is at least shorter (there are only four more lines). What
Pound has done is to redo a Yeatsian experience, using the master's
rhythmical devices, casting over the whole a mood of pre-Raphaelite
suggestiveness, employing an eminently pre-Raphaelite image in the
first stanza, and constructing the second stanza from one image of the
nineties ("The black shadow of your beauty / On the White face of my
beloved") and one from his reading in Provençal ("a-glinting in the
pools of her eyes"). Such a description seems absurd, but the fact is
that the poem, like others in *Exultations*, simply dissolves into its
literary antecedents.

Judging by the extent to which Yeats pervades *Exultations*, it would
seem that Pound was now making the same straightforward study of his
friend's techniques that he was carrying out with Provençal and Tuscan
poetry. Hence the stage Irish of "Planh":

> Out of a new sorrow it is,
> That my hunting hath brought me.
>
>   . . .
>
> But if one should look at me with the old hunger in
>   her eyes,
> How will I be answering her eyes?

If it were not that the theme—the poet's pursuit of Beauty—is an important one in Pound's work at this time, we should suspect that either
our leg or Yeats's was being pulled. Aside from these Irishisms, which
we may hope were not really Pound's idea of Yeats's "Irish rhythms,"
"Planh" is a skillfully close representation of at least one of Yeats's
characteristic genres—the poet perceiving strange, shadowy folk moving
about in some enchanted natural setting where the faery are known to
reside. "Aye!" continues Pound's speaker,

> It's a long hunting
> And it's a deep hunger I have when I see them a-gliding
> And a-flickering there, where the trees stand apart.

This is followed by a typically Yeatsian gesture, the melancholy (and
here rather disattached) summation of the mood of the poem, almost
the moral of the story: "But oh, it is sorrow and sorrow / When love
dies-down in the heart."

Yeats is called upon with equal forthrightness in "Laudantes Decem Pulchritudinis Johannae Templi." We shall see how this poem explores as well the possibilities of Provençal stanza forms—indeed, the poem as a whole is an elaborate kind of dance, moving from one style to another, one rhythm to another, a recital performed by the poet to display his accomplishments to date. The trouble is the same as in "Nils Lykke": Pound comes too close to the Yeatsian manner as practiced by the original owner to be able to draw on it in any creative sense. His nearly outright acknowledgment of his source in part two of this poem does not help:

> I am torn, torn with thy beauty,
> O Rose of the sharpest thorn!
> O Rose of the crimson beauty,
>
>   . . .
>
> O Rose of the crimson thorn.

This is followed immediately by the opening of part three, about "The unappeasable loveliness." And after this tribute to some half a dozen poems in *The Wind among the Reeds*, Pound takes up, in part four, the rhythm of "The Lover Tells of the Rose in His Heart":

> Pale hair that the moon has shaken
> Down over the dark breast of the sea,
> O magic her beauty has shaken
> About the heart of me:
> Out of you have I woven a dream
> That shall walk in the lonely vale.

Such undisguised excursions into the manner of Yeats are carried on throughout *Personae* and *Exultations.* [2]

This, of course, is experiment of a different—we might say lower—

[2] For example, "Search," the song of the "Voices in the Wind" in "Idyl for Glaucus," and "The White Stag." There is an almost direct imitation of the stories and verse of *The Celtic Twilight* in the tenth song of the "Laudantes Decem":

> The glamour of the soul hath come upon me,
> And as the twilight comes upon the roses,
> Walking silently among them,
> So have the thoughts of my heart
> Gone out slowly in the twilight
> Toward my beloved,
> Toward the crimson rose, the fairest.

order from what Pound does with his "studies" of Provençal verse. A few years later he was to distinguish two kinds of literary influence: a poet might be moved to emulation, or "the sight of the work may beget simply a counterfeiting of its superficial qualities. This last is without value, a dodge of the arriviste and of the mere searcher for novelty."[3] This would be too harsh a judgment to make of these last few poems, for the imitation here, to quote the same essay, is "a closer sort of study of the original. Such study may be more 'provocative' than a casual reading, and therefore of value to the artist, so long as it does not impede him in his task of making new and original structures."

This would seem to be the real significance of all these Yeatsian gestures, and the Yeatsian exercises alternate with equally candid experiments in the usages of Decadent poetry, one of which, the opening stanza of "Laudantes Decem," is a "closer sort of study" of Dowson:

> When your beauty is grown old in all men's songs,
> And my poor words are lost amid that throng,
> Then you will know the truth of my poor words,
> And mayhap dreaming of the wistful throng
> That hopeless sigh your praises in their songs,
> You will think kindly then of these mad words.

Pound is very good here at fitting rhythm to mood, even though he does it with someone else's tools. The unobtrusive rhythm is the right accompaniment for the poem's de-energized emotional stance. The repetition of "poor words" threatens too much of a good thing, but the change in the last line to "mad words" avoids oversaturation while it preserves the limp posture of the persona. Part eight also seems to draw upon Dowson. In both cases the rhythm is his, and the low pitch of emotion reflects at least one dimension of his work:

> Because I was idolatrous and have besought,
> With grievous supplication and consuming prayer,
> The admirable image that my dreams have wrought
> Out of her swan's neck and her dark, abundant hair:
> The jealous gods, who brook no worship save their own,
> Turned my live idol marble and her heart to stone.
>
> ("Epigram," *Poetical Works, 57*)

We might hesitate to call such imitation as Pound indulges in here the reflection of influence, were it not that he has evidently learned at least

---

[3] "The Approach to Paris—II," *NA*, XIII (September 11, 1913), 577.

one lesson: note how the rhythm of the Dowson passage undercuts what could otherwise be (and often was) a much stronger emotion. This "Epigram" has a studied dryness about it, as of emotion suppressed, and Pound captures the same mood perfectly. As Dowson undercuts the potential emotionality of "grievous supplication and consuming prayer" by means of deliberately muted rhythm, and as he sidesteps a possibly strong emotion by modifying *image* with the restrained and nonsensual *admirable*, so Pound deliberately saps the vigor of his throng of poets by making them *wistful* and muffles the potential noise of their praising by saying that they "hopeless *sigh* your praises." Originality aside, the poem does a good job of establishing its mood—perhaps too good, given the melodramatic wail that opens the second part with "I am torn, torn with thy beauty, / O Rose of the sharpest thorn!"

The very closeness of these studies makes them seem naive. What I have been referring to as the "mannerisms" of this poet or that are, of course, much more than that. They become mannerisms only when we detach them from the organic complexes of imagery, theme, emotional cast, diction, rhythm, and aural patterns of the poems in which they appear. Failing an absolutely perfect identification between original and imitation, the closer an imitation, the more false or superficial it will seem, for the very closeness will call up by association the other, more subtle features of the complex. At first, therefore, we are inclined to think that for Pound to imitate Yeats and the Decadents as he does in these poems is as silly as attempting to make a tree by patching together various sticks and leaves we have picked up because they seemed to be attractive aspects of trees. There are points at which this kind of tool borrowing shades over into new creation, but to "create" a couplet like "But oh, it is sorrow and sorrow / When love dies-down in the heart" implies a conception of poetry as some kind of warehouse to which a poet may repair for bricks, nuts and bolts, touch-up paint, or what have you. And something very like this underlies these experiments of Pound's, a conception similar to what underlies T. S. Eliot's warning that "To the member of the Browning Study Circle, the discussion of poets about poetry may seem arid, technical, and limited." There were concrete, practical things that Pound had to learn, and close imitation was one kind of training. "You are out of touch," he told Williams, thereby describing his own condition upon his arrival in London. Later, when he spoke of *Personae* as the starting point of his search for self, he was not shoving the excised poems in *A Lume Spento* under the rug, but tacitly acknowledging their limited significance as only a prelude to the work which, in London, he discovered he had to do.

Hugh Kenner

Mauberley

Firmness,
Not the full smile,
His art, but an art
In profile.

With the partial exception of the *Cathay* sequence, the *Personae* volume up to page 183 may be said to be implicit in the *Cantos*. The early poems are deficient in finality; they supplement and correct one another; they stand up individually as renderings of moods, but not as manifestations of mature self-knowledge; they try out poses. They are leading their author somewhere; the reader may be excused if his interests are not wholly engaged, if he finds himself separating the technique from the value of the presented state. This may be said without unsaying anything in the preceding survey, the object of which has been to suggest considerable profit in what may not appear of compelling interest at first glance in 1951. Not only is the history of the purification of our post-Victorian speech contained in those pages, but a right perception of the kinds of achievement these contained will make the *Cantos* easier reading. And in isolating principles of apprehension it has been an advantage to have relatively uncomplicated texts to explicate.

The volume ends, however, with two great self-justifying poems. *Homage to Sextus Propertius* (1917) and *Hugh Selwyn Mauberley* (1920) would, had not a single Canto been finished, dispel any doubt of Pound's being a major poet.

It will be convenient to shorten our discussion by referring the reader to Dr. Leavis' tributes to *Mauberley* in *New Bearings in English Poetry*. That the poem moves him as it does, and that he registers his admiration so adequately and with such economical power of inciting others to comprehension, may, considering the intrinsic resistance of the Bloomsbury-Cambridge milieu to all but certain types of subtly-discriminated moral fervours, be taken as some gauge of the emotional weight, the momentum of essential seriousness, massed in these seventeen pages of disrupted quatrains.

Yet the reader will infer correctly from this way of describing Dr. Leavis' dealings with *Mauberley* that the highly selective vision of that honest and irascible critic has screened out certain essential elements. Pound emerges from his account as a man of one poem; the early work is uninteresting, the *Cantos* a monument of elegant dilettantism. In *Mauberley,* for a few pages, under urgent and unhappily transient personal pressures, he found himself with precision and sincerity. Dr. Leavis' view of Pound's career is introduced here as representative of the most respectable critical thought. Setting aside journalistic opportunism of the kind that has no real concern for letters, attacks on Pound are generally attacks on the *Cantos.* The isolated success of *Mauberley* is generally conceded. The dispraise even of Mr. Winters is qualified somewhat at this point.

Mauberley, that is, is a tricky poem. It is difficult for men of a certain training not to misread it subtly, to select from its elements certain strings that reverberate to an Eliotic tuning fork. A taste for contemporary poetry that has shaped itself almost entirely on Mr. Eliot's resonant introspections has no difficulty in catching what it has come to regard as the sole note of contemporary poetic sincerity in:

> For three years, out of key with his time,
> He strove to resuscitate the dead art
> Of poetry: to maintain "the sublime"
> In the old sense. Wrong from the start—

It is easy to see how this chimes with such passages as:

> So here I am, in the middle way, having had
>   twenty years—

Twenty years largely wasted, the years of *l'entre deux*
    guerres—
Trying to learn to use words, and every attempt
Is a wholly new start, and a different kind of failure
Because one has only learnt to get the better of words
For the thing one no longer has to say, or the way in which
One is no longer disposed to say it . . .
                                            "East Coker," V

It may briefly be said that there has been a muddle about "impersonality." Mr. Eliot's impersonality is Augustinian; a dispassionate contemplation of the self which permits without romantic impurities a poetic corpus of metamorphosed personae. Pound's impersonality is Flaubertian: an effacement of the personal accidents of the perceiving medium in the interests of accurate registration of *moeurs contemporaines.* As we have said, the adoption of various personae is for such an artist merely a means to ultimate depersonalization, ancillary and not substantial to his major work. J. Alfred Prufrock is not Mr. Eliot, but he speaks with Mr. Eliot's voice and bears intricate analogical relations with the later Eliot persona who is the speaker of *Four Quartets.* Hugh Selwyn Mauberley, on the other hand, does not speak with Mr. Pound's voice, and is more antithetically than intimately related to the poet of the *Cantos.* It would be misleading to say that he is a portion of Mr. Pound's self whom Mr. Pound is externalizing in order to get rid of him (like Stephen Dedalus); it would be a more accurate exaggeration to say that he is a parody of Pound the poet with whom Mr. Pound is anxious not to be confounded.

The sort of critic we have been mentioning, the one who finds the note of sincerity in *Mauberley* as nowhere else in Pound, pays unconscious tribute to the accuracy with which Pound, in quest of devices for articulating this quasi-Prufrockian figure, has echoed the intonations and gestures of a characteristic Eliot poem.[1] Such a critic has been known to quote in confirmation of his view of Pound Mr. Eliot's remark, "I am sure of *Mauberley*, whatever else I am sure of." Mr. Eliot has not, however, the perceptive limitations of his disciples; in the same essay he insists that the entire *Personae* collection is to be read as a process of exploration leading up to the *Cantos,* "which are wholly himself."

It may be helpful to remark that Joyce is in this respect like Pound, an artist of the Flaubertian kind; his Stephen Dedalus is a parody of himself, not an artist but an aesthete, at length mercilessly ridiculed in *Finnegan's Wake.* The analogy is reasonably exact; Stephen is partly an aspect of Joyce himself which Joyce is trying to purify; his horror of

[1] The primary echo is as a matter of fact with Corbière.

bourgeois civilization echoes Joyce's much as *Mauberley's* "sense of graduations,"

> Quite out of place amid
> Resistance of current exacerbations,

echoes Pound's. But Joyce refrains from unambiguous sympathy with Stephen's desire for Shelleyan sunward flight; he involves Stephen in an Icarian fall into the sea of matter just as Pound reduces Mauberley to

> Nothing, in brief, but maudlin confession,
> Irresponse to human aggression,
> Amid the precipitation, down-float
> Of insubstantial manna,
> Lifting the faint susurrus
> Of his subjective hosannah.

This cannot be taken as an account of the poet of the *Cantos* any more than Stephen's fastidious shrinking away from common noises can be regarded as characteristic of the author of *Ulysses.* Both men channelled their disgust into patient sifting of immense sottisiers; Pound has been, significantly, almost alone in perceiving the continuity between *Ulysses* and *Bouvard et Pécuchet.* In *Ulysses* Stephen is the focus of spectacular technical sonorities, sympathized with and rejected; the same is true of the Lotus-eaters in the *Cantos.*

It may be remarked that the critic who thinks of *Mauberley* as Pound's one successful poem commonly sees Stephen Dedalus as the hero of *Ulysses*, perceives in both figures elements of failure, and takes as dim a view of Joyce as of the author of the *Cantos.*

Against what may be mistaken for the drift of the above paragraphs, it should be insisted that the process of creating and disowning Hugh Selwyn Mauberley had not the personal importance for Pound that the purgation of the Dedalian aspects of himself had for Joyce. No such trauma was involved in the Idaho poet's flight from America as in the Irish novelist's disentanglement from Church and Motherland. It is not true, on the other hand, to say that Joyce could do nothing until he had focused and gotten rid of Stephen: the bulk of *Dubliners* was written in 1904, in Joyce's twenty-third year. But even when we have balanced *Dubliners* with the social observations in *Lustra,* and *Chamber Music* with the first volume of *Personae,* the excernment of Stephen Dedalus remains of crucial importance to Joyce's future achievement in a way that the writing of *Mauberley* probably was not to Pound. It was probably necessary that he focus in some such oblique way the tension

between popular demands and his earlier poetic activities before em-
barking on the *Cantos;* but the process need not be thought to have
coincided with a spiritual crisis from which, as it suits the critic, he
emerged either crippled or annealed.

Mauberley does not mark in that way a hurt awakening from
aesthetic playgrounds into thin cruel daylight. Its postures and conflicts
continue, as we have indicated, those of *Propertius,* the *robustezza*
of which could scarcely be confounded with hurt awakening.[2] If a
decisive point of maturation must be found, it is to be found in
Propertius, the earlier poem, it is not always remembered, by some
three years. It is easy, for that matter, to over-estimate the reorientation there involved *vis-a-vis* the earlier work. There need be nothing
traumatic about supervening maturity; the bulk of *Personae* is the work
of a young man in his twenties. Pound was born in 1885. The earliest
Personae, dated 1908, belong therefore to *ætat.* 23. He published the
Seafarer translation at 27; *Lustra* at 30, *Cathay* at 31. The next year
saw *Propertius* and the first drafts of the earliest cantos. He published
Mauberley at 35. The *Pisan Cantos* are the work of a man of 60.
Emotional maturation may be seen going on in the *Lustra* volume; and
there is enough difference between the monolinear intensity of "The
Needle" (*Ripostes,* 1912):

> Come, or the stellar tide will slip away,
> Eastward avoid the hour of its decline,
> Now! for the needle trembles in my soul! ...

and the calm detached emotion of "Gentildonna" (*Lustra,* 1915):

> She passed and left no quiver in the veins, who now
> Moving among the trees, and clinging
>   in the air she severed,
> Fanning the grass she walked on then, endures:
> Grey oil leaves beneath a rain-cold sky.

to preclude any suggestion of a cataclysmic reorientation a few years
later.

These pages will have performed their function if they can arm the
reader against the too-easy supposition that Pound found in *Mauberley*
an eloquence of disillusion. The subtle balance of diverse strong emotions
in that poem will be utterly destroyed by too ready a response to one or

---

[2]Since writing this I find in Pound's recently published *Letters* a reference to
Mauberley as essentially a popularization of *Propertius;* though the context indi-
cates Pound's awareness that this is not the whole story.

two elements. We may now look, belatedly, at the text.

The subtitle ("Life and Contacts") and the title-page footnote (". . . distinctly a farewell to London") furnished a perspective on the title of the first of the eighteen poems: "E. P. Ode Pour L'Election de son Sepulchre."[3] This is largely Pound's career in London seen through the eyes of uncomprehending but not unsympathetic conservers of the "better tradition": a strenuous but ineffectual angel, his subtleties of passion "wrong from the start," accorded the patronizing excuse of having been born "in a half savage country, out of date," and given to Yankee intensities ("bent resolutely on wringing lilies from the acorn") of an unclubbable sort. The epitaph modulates into grudging admiration for the pertinacity of this dedicated spirit—

> His true Penelope was Flaubert,
> He fished by obstinate isles;
> Observed the elegance of Circe's hair
> Rather than the mottoes on sun-dials.

The first line of this stanza renders with astonishing concision an intricate set of cultural perspectives. Pound's voyages to China, to Tuscany, to Provence, his battles with Polyphemic editors and his dallyings with pre-Raphaelite Sirens, are transformed, as in the *Cantos,* into an Odyssey of discovery and frustration, imposed, for jealous and irrelevant reasons, by the ruler of the seas (a neat fusion of the chaotic state of letters with English mercantile smugness; the "obstinate isles" are both the British Isles and recalcitrant aesthetic objectives.) The irony with which the British mortician of reputations is made to utter unambiguous truths about artistic effort (cf. the "Beauty is difficult" motif of the *Pisan Cantos)* at the same time as he vaunts his national obstinacy and imperception, is carried on with the mention of Flaubert, the "true Penelope" of this voyage. For Pound, Flaubert is the true (=faithful) counterpart, entangling crowds of suitors (superficial "realists") in their own self-deceit while she awaits the dedicated partner whose arm can bend the hard bow of the "Mot Juste." Flaubert represents the ideal of disciplined self-immolation from which English poetry has been too long estranged, only to be rejoined by apparently circuitous voyaging. For the writer of the epitaph, on the other hand, Flaubert is conceded to be E. P.'s "true"

[3] A line of Ronsard, connected by Pound with the *Epitaphe* of Corbière, to whose procedures *Mauberley* is related as early Eliot is related to Laforgue. At the time when *Mauberley* was written, Eliot was getting rid of Laforgue and in collaboration with Pound assimilating Corbière and Gautier. The Corbière reverberations are functional in Pound's poem, relating it to still more complex modes of self-knowledge than we have opportunity to go into here. At its deepest levels the poem is still virtually unread.

(=equivalent) Penelope only in deprecation: Flaubert being for the English literary mind of the first quarter of the present century a foreign, feminine, rather comically earnest indulger in quite un-British preciosity; "wrong from the start," surrounded by mistaken admirers, and very possibly a whore; a suitable Penelope for this energetic American. England was at that time preparing to burn and ban *Ulysses* exactly as France had sixty years before subjected *Madame Bovary* to juridical process; it was the complaint of the tribunal against Flaubert that he had spent pains on the elegance of his Circe's hair that might better have been diverted to honester causes.

The implications of line after line, irony upon irony, might be expanded in this way; the epitaph concludes with a superbly categorical dismissal of this *impetuus juventus* from the cadres of responsible literary position:

> Unaffected by "the march of events,"
> He passed from men's memory in *l'an trentiesme*
> *De son eage;* the case presents
> No adjunct to the Muse's diadem.

The echo of Villon is of course the crowning irony. *His* passage from the memory of his contemporaries has if anything augmented his place in the history of poetry.

As soon as we see that this epitaph is not (except at the level at which it transposes Corbière) being written by Pound, the entire sequence falls into focus. The eleven succeeding poems (II-XII) present an ideogrammic survey of the cultural state of post-war England: of the culture which we have just heard pronouncing upon the futility of Pound's effort to "resuscitate the dead art of poetry." The artist who was "unaffected by the march of events" offers his version of this criterion:

> The age demanded an image
> Of its accelerated grimace;

the third poem, with its audacious closing counterpoint from Pindar's *Second Olympic* (of which there is a readily accessible translation in the *Biographia Literaria,* ch. xviii), generalizes with a more austere bitterness:

> All things are a flowing,
> Sage Heracleitus says;
> But a tawdry cheapness
> Shall outlast our days.

Poems IV and V are similarly paired. IV surveys with compassion the moral dilemmas of the war:

> These fought in any case,
> and some believing,
>   pro domo, in any case . . .

poises sacrifice against domestic cheapness:

> walked eye-deep in hell
> believing in old men's lies, then unbelieving
> came home, home to a lie,
> home to many deceits,
> home to old lies and new infamy;
> usury age-old and age-thick
> and liars in public places.

and closes with a quick evocation of the pullulating new artistic soil, entrapping the artist in an opportunity for defined and significant passions that all but swamp his Flaubertian criteria:

> frankness as never before,
> disillusions as never told in the old days,
> hysterias, trench confessions,
> laughter out of dead bellies.

Poem V intensifies the antithesis between sacrifice and gain:

> Charm, smiling at the good mouth,
> Quick eyes gone under earth's lid,
>
> For two gross of broken statues,
> For a few thousand battered books.

The cultural heritage has been reduced to the status of a junkman's inventory by the conservators of tradition mobilized behind the epitaph of poem I; the superimposed tension of the apparent incommensurability, at best, of human lives and civilized achievements brings the sequence to a preliminary climax that prepares for the change of the next six sections into a retrospective key.

"Yeux Glauques" poises the pre-Raphaelite purity,

> Thin like brook water,
> With a vacant gaze

against the bustle of Gladstone and Buchanan (whose attack on "The Fleshly School of Poetry" was answered by Rossetti and Swinburne). The painted woman of the poem contains in her "questing and passive" gaze the complex qualities of passion, between the poles of Swinburne and Burne-Jones, which the aesthetic movement of the nineteenth century mobilized against a world in which "The English Rubaiyat was still-born." The picturesque reminiscences of the nineties in the next poem intensify the personal tragedies of the inheritors of that movement; "Dowson found harlots cheaper than hotels." This struggle and rebuttal is, we see, still being carried on; a new dimension of tradition and conflict is added to the efforts of the epitaphed E. P. of the first poem. The success of official literary history in discrediting the vitality of the century of Rossetti, Swinburne, and Fitzgerald and turning it instead into the century of Ruskin, Carlyle, and Tennyson is epitomized in the final stanza:

> M. Verog, out of step with the decade,
> Detached from his contemporaries,
> Neglected by the young,
> Because of these reveries.

M. Verog, "author of *The Dorian Mood*," is a pseudonym for Victor Plarr, who appears in Canto LXXIV "talking of mathematics." The next three poems are vignettes of three contrasting literary careers. "Brennbaum" (? Max Beerbohm) embodies what passes for the cult of "style":

> The stiffness from spats to collar
> Never relaxing into grace.

This style is neo-classical, not that of the leaping arch; Brennbaum's motive is simply to prepare a face to meet the faces that he meets; such emotional intensity as he knows is not only repressed almost to imperceptibility, its dynamic is private, alien, and accidental to the traditions of Latin Europe: "The heavy memories of Horeb, Sinai, and the forty years."

Mr. Nixon, exhibit number two, is the successful public man of letters (? Arnold Bennett). The forced rhymes (reviewer/you are) enact his hearty grimaces; his drawled climactic maxim,

> . . . as for literature
> It gives no man a sinecure,

unites the pretentious popular philosophy of a Wells, a Shaw, a Bennett with the smug generalizations of commercial success and the hard-boiled saws of *Poor Richard's Almanac.*

> "And give up verse, my boy,
> "There's nothing in it."

The third exhibit is the genuine stylist in hiding, an anticlimactic redaction of "The Lake Isle of Innisfree":

> The haven from sophistications and contentions
> Leaks through its thatch;
> He offers succulent cooking;
> The door has a creaking latch.

These are not *poèmes à clef*; but the post-war fortunes of Ford Madox Ford are entirely apropos. Ford, the collaborator of Conrad and in the decade pre-war the lone enunciator of the Flaubertian gospel in England, on his discharge from the army retired in disgust to Sussex to raise pigs, and ultimately, at about the same time as Pound, left England. His detailed account of the cultural state of post-war London in the first third of *It Was the Nightingale* can be made to document *Mauberley* line by line. The reviewing synod hastened to write his epitaph, so effectively that his reputation is only beginning to quicken a quarter of a century after the publication of his best work. Pound has never made a secret of his respect for Ford, and Ford has testified that Pound alone of the young writers he could claim to have "discovered" about 1908 did not amid his later misfortunes disown and castigate him. It pleases at least one reader to suppose that it is the spectacle of Ford's disillusion that animates these three extraordinary stanzas.

Poems XI and XII present a post-war contrast to the intricate contemplative passion of "Yeux Glauques." The twelfth closes the survey of the London situation with an image of grotesquely effusive aristocratic patronage; "Daphne with her thighs in bark" dwindles to the Lady Valentine in her stuffed-satin drawing-room, dispensing "well-gowned approbation of literary effort" in sublime assurance of her vocation for a career of taste and discrimination:

> Poetry, her border of ideas,
> The edge, uncertain, but a means of blending
> With other strata
> Where the lower and higher have ending;

> A hook to catch the Lady Jane's attention,
> A modulation toward the theatre,
> Also, in the case of revolution,
> A possible friend and comforter.

Dr. Johnson's letter to Lord Chesterfield stands as the archetypal repudiation of the vague, vain, and irrelevant claims of patronage; but the street of literary commerce to which Johnson turned has also lost its power to support the artist:

> Beside this thoroughfare
> The sale of half-hose has
> Long since superseded the cultivation
> Of Pierian roses.

The *Envoi* which follows is a consummate ironic climax; against these squalors is asserted the audacious Shakespearean vocation of preserving transient beauty against the tooth of time (cf. the end of the first *Propertius* poem); against the halting and adroitly short-winded quatrains of the "dumb-born book" is set a magnificently sustained melodic line:

> Go, dumb-born book,
> Tell her that sang me once that song of Lawes:
> Hadst thou but song
> As thou hast subjects known,
> Then were there cause in thee that should condone
> Even my faults that heavy upon me lie,
> And build her glories their longevity. . . .

Seventeenth-century music, the union of poetry with song, immortal beauty, vocalic melody, treasure shed on the air, transcend for a single page the fogs and squabbles of the preceding sections in a poem that ironically yearns for the freedom and power which it displays in every turn of phrase, in triumphant vindication of those years of fishing by obstinate isles. The poet who was buried in the first section amid such deprecation rises a Phoenix to confront his immolators, asserting the survival of at least this song

> When our two dusts with Waller's shall be laid,
> Siftings on siftings in oblivion,
> Till change hath broken down
> All things save Beauty alone.

There follows a five-part coda in which the Mauberley *persona* comes to the fore; gathering up the motifs of the earlier sections, the enigmatic stanzas mount from intensity to intensity to chronicle the death of the Jamesian hero who might have been Pound. Part two is practically a précis of the flirtation with passionate illusion of Lambert Strether in *The Ambassadors.* "Of course I moved among miracles," said Strether. "It was all phantasmagoric." The third part contains the essential action; having postulated Mauberley's "fundamental passion":

> This urge to convey the relation
> Of eye-lid and cheek-bone
> By verbal manifestations;
>
> To present the series
> Of curious heads in medallion,

and implied a context of opportunities missed—

> Which anaesthesis, noted a year late,
> And weighed, revealed his great affect,
> (Orchid), mandate
> Of Eros, a retrospect.

—Pound particularizes on the Propertian conflict between the aesthetic martyr and the demands of the age.

Contemplation is weighed against Shavian strenuousness:

> The glow of porcelain
> Brought no reforming sense
> To his perception
> Of the social inconsequence.
>
> Thus if her colour
> Came against his gaze,
> Tempered as if
> It were through a perfect glaze
>
> He made no immediate application
> Of this to relation of the state
> To the individual, the month was more temperate
> Because this beauty had been.

In Canto XIII Confucius provides a cross-light:

> And Kung raised his cane against Yuan Jang,
>   Yuan Jang being his elder,

> For Yuan Jang sat by the roadside pretending to
>   be receiving wisdom.
> And Kung said
>   "You old fool, come out of it,
> Get up and do something useful."

The serious artist does not "pretend to be receiving wisdom"; we have heard Pound dilating on his quasi-automatic social functions. It is the essence of the artist's cruel dilemma that his just reaction against politicians' and journalists' canons of usefulness drives him so perilously close to

> . . . an Olympian *apathein*
> In the presence of selected perceptions.[4]

The descent into this Nirvana of the fastidious moth with the previously-cadenced name is chronicled with elaborate subtlety. The validity of his perceptions is played off against "neo-Nietzschean clatter," but meanwhile the directness of the opening images, the red-beaked steeds, the glow of porcelain, is being gradually overlaid by a crescendo of abstractions: "isolation," "examination," "elimination," "consterna-tion," "undulation," "concentration." The tone shifts from the sympa-thetic to the clinical:

> Invitation, mere invitation to perceptivity
> Gradually led him to the isolation
> Which these presents place
> Under a more tolerant, perhaps, examination.

The preservation of a critical distance both from the inadequacies of Mauberley and from the irrelevantly active world of Mr. Nixon, Nietzsche, and Bishop Bloughram, with its "discouraging doctrine of chances," the realization of an impersonality that extracts strength from both of the antithetical cadres of the first twelve poems, is the major achievement of these final pages. Mauberley's disappearance into his

---

[4] It should be noted that the *Pisan Cantos* derive their extraordinary vitality from the fact that an *apathein* among memorably-rendered "selected perceptions" is not being crudely opposed, in H. S. Mauberley's fashion, to the "current exacer-bations," of the prison-camp. The moon-nymph, the lynxes, the Chinese sages, the healing rain, unite with the gun-roosts and the dialogue of murderers to form new perceptive wholes. Pound's "armor against utter consternation" is not gotten "by constant elimination" but by vigorous fusion. The *Pisan Cantos* comment on *Mauberley* in a way Pound furthered by incorporating plangent scraps of the earlier poem into Canto LXXIV.

dream-world is related without approbation and without scorn:

> A pale gold, in the aforesaid pattern,
> The unexpected palms
> Destroying, certainly, the artist's urge,
> Left him delighted with the imaginary
> Audition of the phantasmal sea-surge,

and we are warned by inverted commas in the next stanza against adopting too readily the standpoint of pontifical criticism:

> Incapable of the least utterance or composition,
> Emendation, conservation of the "better tradition,"
> Refinement of medium, elimination of superfluities,
> August attraction or concentration.

That "better tradition" interjects the accent of a Buchanan or an Edmund Gosse; the other canons are Flaubertian. Mauberley is not simply a failure by Mr. Nixon's standards of success, he is a failure *tout court;* he is the man to whom that initial epitaph might with justice be applied; the man for whom the writer of the epitaph has mistaken "E. P." It is the focusing of this that guarantees the closing irony:

> Ultimate affronts to
> Human redundancies;
>
> Non-esteem of self-styled "his betters"
> Leading, as he well knew,
> To his final
> Exclusion from the world of letters.

The irrelevancy of the canons of "the world of letters," for once right but from utterly wrong reasons, very efficient in guillotining the already defunct, could not be more subtly indicated.

As a technical marvel this poem cannot be too highly praised. Only Pound's economical means were sufficiently delicate for the discriminations he sought to effect: "perhaps" and "we admit" belong to one mode of perception, "the month was more temperate because this beauty had been" to another, the concessive "certainly" and the clinical "incapable" and "in brief" to a third. The technique of distinguishing motivations and qualities of insight solely by scrupulous groupings of notes on the connotative or etymological keyboard has never been brought to greater refinement. One cannot think of another poet who could have brought it off.

The sequence is re-focused by a vignette of hedonistic drift protracting the coral island imagery that had troubled Mauberley's reverie, ending with an epitaph scrawled on an oar,

> "I was
> And I no more exist;
> Here drifted
> An hedonist."

pathetic echo of the elaborate opening "Ode Pour L'Election de son Sepulchre." The final "Medallion," to be balanced against the "Envoi" of the first part, recurs in witty disenchantment to the singing lady. Neither the Envoi's passion:

> Tell her that sheds
> Such treasure on the air,
> Recking naught else but that her graces give
> Life to the moment . . .

nor Mauberley's "porcelain reverie":

> Thus if her colour
> Came against his gaze,
> Tempered as if
> It were through a perfect glaze

is denied by the paradoxical dispassion of the final picture:

> Luini in porcelain!
> The grand piano
> Utters a profane
> Protest with her clean soprano.

But the tone is "objective" in a way that detaches the "Medallion" from the claims of the various worlds of perception projected in earlier parts of the poem. There are witty echoes of those worlds: the "profane protest" of heavy-fingered clubbably professional letters;[5] an ambrosial Mauberleian dream of braids

> Spun in King Minos' hall
> From metal, or intractable amber;

[5]Cf. "as the young horse whinnies against the tubas" (Canto LXXIX).

but the closing stanza is pitched to a key of quasi-scientific meticulous-
ness that delivers with Flaubertian inscrutability a last voiceless verdict
of inadequacy on all the human squinting, interpreting, and colouring
that has preceded: fact revenging itself on art and the artists—

> The face-oval beneath the glaze,
> Bright in its suave bounding-line, as,
> Beneath half-watt rays,
> The eyes turn topaz.

Beauty? Irony? Geometrical and optical fact?

And this last poem yields a final irony. "To present the series/Of
curious heads in medallion" was, we remember, Mauberley's ambition,
and this sample Medallion in its very scrupulousness exemplifies his
sterility. His imagination falls back upon precedents; his visual particu-
larity comes out of an art-gallery and his Venus Anadyomene out of a
book. The "true Penelope" of both poets was Flaubert, but Pound's
contrasting Envoi moves with authority of another order. Mauberley
cringed before the age's demands; he wrote one poem and collapsed.
Pound with sardonic compliance presents the age with its desiderated
"image" (poems 3-12); then proves he was *right* from the start by offering as indisputable climax the "sculpture of rhyme" and the "sublime
in the old sense" which the epitaph-writer had dismissed as a foolish
quest. And he adds a sympathetic obituary and epitaph of his own for
the *alter ego.*

This thin-line tracing of the action of *Mauberley* is offered with no
pretense to fullness. It is possible, as we have seen, to spend a page
meditating on a line. The writer professes two objectives in proceeding
as above. First, it seemed profitable to trace the "intaglio method"
through an entire work, with a detail which will be impossible when we
come to the *Cantos.* Secondly, it seemed important to guide the reader
towards an apprehension of *Mauberley* in terms that will not falsify his
notion of Pound's later or earlier work. The poem has commended
itself too readily as a memorable confession of failure to those whom
it comforts to decide that Pound has failed. Anyone to whom the above
pages are persuasive will perhaps agree that a less obvious perspective
augments, if anything, the stature of this astonishing poem.

Donald Davie

The Pisan Cantos

In an interesting passage from *Modern Painters* (vol. IV, ch. xx) Ruskin speaks of "the kind of admiration with which a southern artist regarded the *stone* he worked in; and the pride which populace or priest took in the possession of precious mountain substance, worked into the pavements of their cathedrals, and the shafts of their tombs." Thus to regard the worked stone as "mountain substance," and to assert that the Italians thus regarded it, is to move at once into the area of interest of Adrian Stokes and to Canto 17. And it is significant that to illustrate his point Ruskin quotes aptly from "The Bishop Orders His Tomb in St. Praxed's Church" by the poet, Browning, whom Pound has never ceased to honor as one of his first masters—"pourquoi nier son père?" Taking into account some of Pound's even less fashionable allegiances, for example, to Ford Madox Ford and to Whistler, it would not be hard to trace for him a direct line of descent from Ruskin.

But this is hardly worth doing where the affinities are in any case so many and so clear. G. S. Fraser, for instance, considering Pound's position as a thinker about society, very justly sees it as Ruskinian:

"By their fruits ye shall know them." There must be something right about the society that produces Chartres and something wrong that produces, say London south of the river. Men like Adams and

From Ezra Pound: Poet as Sculptor, *by Donald Davie (New York: Oxford University Press, 1964). Copyright © 1964 by Donald Davie. Reprinted by permission of Oxford University Press, Inc., and Routledge and Kegan Paul, Ltd.*

Jefferson respect the arts, but they are not in Mauberley's sense "aesthetes," and indeed throughout *The Cantos* Pound seems to be moving away from Mauberley's still faintly ninetyish attitude towards one more like Ruskin's in *Unto this Last*; it must be good men, in a good society, who build a good cathedral.[1]

Rather plainly Fraser feels that the relationship between healthy art and healthy society is somehow more complicated than this. And one may agree with him, while still applauding both Pound and Ruskin for asserting that *some* connection there must be, and a close one, too. This is the less satisfactory side of Ruskin, just as, in the long run, it is the frightening and repellent side of Pound. Both men, who are very wise about trees and swans, mountains and skies and clouds, wasps and ants ("And now the ants seem to stagger/as the dawn sun has trapped their shadows"—Canto 83), and about buildings and paintings and bas-reliefs, become rather dangerously unwise—in particular, unwisely too sure of themselves—when they move, as they are right to do, to regarding the conduct of men in societies. This tragic discontinuity runs, perhaps, through the whole Ruskinian tradition; Gerard Manley Hopkins, for instance, who belongs in this tradition, is much less wise about bugler-boys than he is about highland burns and windhovers.

But in the much more persuasive matter of how they regard the world of human artifacts, Ruskin and Pound represent, each in his own period, a traditional wisdom much older than nineteenth-century romanticism. Mr. Fraser goes on:

> The odd thing is that in religion Pound is a kind of eighteenth-century deist (one of his literary heroes, and an oddly assorted set they are, is Voltaire), and there must be a sense in which the cathedral, and the whole outer fabric of mediaeval life that he loves so passionately, is nothing for him but an adorable mockery or a beautiful empty shell. Critics have noted, and very rightly, the new and very moving note of religious humility in the "Pull down thy vanity" passage in the *Pisan Cantos*; but none of them have noted that the divinity not exactly invoked but hinted at there—the deity that sheathes a blade of grass more elegantly than a Parisian dressmaker sheathes a beautiful woman—is just the divinity of the Deists: Nature, or Nature's God, it hardly matters which one calls it, for it is just enough of a God to keep Nature running smoothly. . . . (*Vision and Rhetoric*, p. 91)

It was Yeats who in the 1920's struck off, in a brilliant phrase already

[1]G. S. Fraser, *Vision and Rhetoric* (London, 1959), pp. 90-91.

quoted, this sympathy for the eighteenth century which is constant
with Pound:

> Ezra Pound arrived the other day, . . . and being warned by his wife
> tried to be very peaceable but couldn't help being very litigious
> about Confucius who I consider should have worn an Eighteenth
> Century wig and preached in St. Paul's, and he thinks the perfect
> man.[2]

Chinese thought, pre-eminently Confucian thought, was introduced to
the West by representatives of the European Enlightenment, and Pound
is devoted to it as were those earliest translators; partly what Pound
does with it is to read back into ancient Chinese an Enlightenment
scheme of things. Similarly Jefferson, together with the whole American
culture that he and other Founding Fathers stand for in the *Cantos*, is
for Pound an Enlightenment product; Jefferson's personality and way
of life exemplify the ideals of a Goldsmith or a Montesquieu. What is
more, Pound's whole philosophy of history is in the strictest sense
"Augustan"; that is to say, like Pope and Swift (but not Addison) he
sees the course of human history in terms of prolonged "dark ages" interrupted by tragically brief luminous islands of achieved civilization,
for which the Rome of Augustus stands as the type. (Pound's very
marked preference for the Roman as against the Greek culture is another
aspect of his Augustanism). Like Pope at the end of the *Dunciad*, Pound
has written and acted as if the precarious islands of achieved civility
were maintained only by unremitting vigilance on the part of a tiny
minority, typically a group of friends, who must continually (and in the
end, always vainly) stop up the holes in the dikes against which the sea
of human stupidity, anarchy, and barbarism washes incessantly. In fact,
if Pound's loyalty to the Enlightenment is taken seriously, most (though
not all) of his other interests and commitments fall into a rationally
coherent, massive, and impressive pattern; and his "literary heroes" will
appear to be much less of "an oddly assorted set."

His mediaevalism, and also that element in him that may be called
"Ruskinian," look rather different if related to a prime controlling sympathy with the Enlightenment. Fraser, for instance, is very just and perceptive about the passage he refers to from Canto 81:

> The ant's a centaur in his dragon world.
> Pull down thy vanity, it is not man
> Made courage, or made order, or made grace,

[2] *The Letters of W. B. Yeats*, ed. Allan Wade (New York, 1955), p. 774.

> Pull down thy vanity, I say pull down.
> Learn of the green world what can be thy place
> In scaled invention or true artistry,
> Pull down thy vanity,
>   Paquin pull down!
> The green casque has outdone your elegance.

The feeling and import of this is indeed, as Fraser suggests, very close to Pope's:

> Far as Creation's ample range extends,
> The scale of sensual, mental pow'rs ascends:
> Mark how it mounts, to Man's imperial race,
> From the green myriads in the peopled grass:
> What modes of sight betwixt each wide extreme,
> The mole's dim curtain, and the lynx's beam:
> Of smell, the headlong lioness between,
> And hound sagacious on the tainted green:
> Of hearing, from the life that fills the flood,
> To that which warbles thro' the vernal wood:
> The spider's touch, how exquisitely fine!
> Feels at each thread, and lives along the line: . . .

"The ant's a centaur in his dragon world" is as near as Pound chooses to come to what interests Pope centrally, the idea of a ladder and of the Great Chain of Being with never a link missing. Faithful to his manifesto in *Gaudier-Brzeska*, and along with Hopkins and Ruskin, Pound's attention has shifted somewhat from this grand design to the tight "designs" achieved on a smaller scale, which the natural world throws up momentarily and incessantly. All the same, Nature is still seen primarily as a designer, and for just this reason is wittily described as a "couturier" in Canto 80:

> as the young lizard extends his leopard spots
>   along the grass-blade seeking the green midge half an ant-size
>
> and the Serpentine will look just the same
> and the gulls be as neat on the pond
> and the sunken garden unchanged
> and God knows what else is left of our London
>   my London, your London
> and if her green elegance
>   remains on this side of my rain ditch
>   puss lizard will lunch on some other T-bone
>
> sunset grand couturier.

It is easy in fact to be so aware of the difference between Pope on the one hand, Ruskin and Hopkins on the other, as to miss the essential identity of their concerns. This is true at least of the Pope of the *Essay on Man* that prompted Ruskin to write of "the serene and just benevolence which placed Pope, in his theology, two centuries in advance of his time."[3] And it was Ruskin who memorably clinched and explained the difference between his interest in nature, and Pope's: "exactly in proportion as the idea of definite spiritual presence in material nature was lost, the mysterious sense of unaccountable life in the things themselves would be increased."[4] As the conviction of an abiding Presence is lost, so the observer expects all the more urgently "presences." Pound manifests this loss of faith, as do Hopkins and Ruskin and, for that matter, Wordsworth. Nevertheless, the essential similarity with Pope remains, between "the green midge half an ant-size" and "the green myriads in the peopled grass." These perceptions are possible only in an attitude of humility about the place of the human in relation to the non-human creation. And it was the shock of Pound's appalling predicament in the American prison-camp in 1945, awaiting trial for treason, that restored to him this humility, after the steady crescendo of raucous arrogance through the Chinese History and American History cantos of the years before.

It may be said that W. B. Yeats shares with the symbolist poets, and with a poet squarely in their tradition, such as T. S. Eliot, an imperious, appropriating attitude toward the perceived world. When swans get into Yeats's verse, the swan loses all its swanliness except what it needs to symbolize something in the person who observes it: "Another emblem there!" And the poet at the end of "Coole Park and Ballylee" says explicitly that this is also what has happened to Lady Gregory. Similarly, Frank Kermode has demonstrated how far "In Memory of Major Robert Gregory" is concerned with Major Gregory, much less for what he is or was in himself than for what the poet chooses to make him stand for in his (the poet's) private pantheon. It is for this reason, to give an example, that Gregory's activities as a landscape painter are made so salient—so that Yeats may applaud this imperious attitude to the natural world at just the point where it would seem least likely, in landscape painting:

> We dreamed that a great painter had been born
> To cold Clare rock and Galway rock and thorn,

[3] John Ruskin, *Lectures on Art* (Oxford, 1870), para. 70.
[4] Quoted by Maynard Mack, Introduction to *An Essay on Man* (Twickenham Edition of the Poems of Pope, Vol. III-i), p. lxxv—where the context is immediately apposite and illuminating.

> To that stern colour and that delicate line
> That are our secret discipline
> Wherein the gazing heart doubles her might.

We attend to natural landscape, not for the sake of delighting in it, nor for what it may tell us of supernatural purpose or design, but so that the imperious personality, seeing itself there reflected, may become the more conscious of its own power—"the gazing heart doubles her might." As Marion Witt was first to show, Yeats intends here to relate Gregory's practice as a landscape painter with that of Samuel Palmer and Edward Calvert, the nineteenth-century artists who, true to the Blakean tradition, which was Yeats's tradition also, reject the discipline that is the scientist's as much as the artist's, exact and intent observation, setting up instead the discipline of the visionary, who sees through the perceivable to what lies beyond.

This is a matter not of mutually exclusive categories but only of where the emphasis characteristically falls. For examples of vivid and exact observation can, of course, be found in Yeats the visionary; and conversely Ezra Pound, who characteristically sees scientific observation as not at all at odds with the poet's kind of attention, also shows himself sympathetic to the Platonist John Heydon ("Secretary of Nature, J. Heydon," in Canto 91) who attends to natural appearances only so as to read them as "signatures" of the realm of essence. The point is best made, therefore, by quotation from Canto 83:

> and Brother Wasp is building a very neat house
> of four rooms, one shaped like a squat indian bottle
> La vespa, *la* vespa, mud, swallow system
> So that dreaming of Bracelonde and of Perugia
> and the great fountain in the Piazza
> or of old Bulagaio's cat that with a well timed leap
> could turn the lever-shaped door handle
> It comes over me that Mr. Walls must be a ten-strike
> with the signorinas
> and in the warmth after chill sunrise
> an infant, green as new grass,
> has stuck its head or tip
> out of Madame La Vespa's bottle
>
> mint springs up again
> in spite of Jones' rodents
> as had the clover by the gorilla cage
> with a four-leaf

When the mind swings by a grass-blade
    an ant's forefoot shall save you
the clover leaf smells and tastes as its flower

The infant has descended
    from mud on the tent roof to Tellus,
like to like colour he goes amid grass-blades
    greeting them that dwell under XTHONOS $X\Theta ONO\Sigma$
*OI X*Θ*ONIOI*; to carry our news
    εἰς χθονιους to them that dwell under the earth,
begotten of air, that shall sing in the bower
    of Kore,   Περσεφόνεια
and have speech with Tiresias, Thebae

If we say that neither Yeats nor Eliot could have written this passage,
we should have in mind, not in the first place any question of poetic
method or strategy, but the quality of the sensibility, the sort of attitude
and attention to the natural world, that is here displayed. It is not
helpful to recall Wordsworth and "a heart/That watches and receives,"
for this sort of contemplation is as much an active participation of the
mind as are the more imperious operations of a Yeats.[5] One is reminded
rather of passages in Coleridge's and Ruskin's notebooks, in some of the
letters of Keats, in the essays and poems of D. H. Lawrence, above all
in the writings of Hopkins. In fact, what lies behind a passage such as
this (and they occur throughout the *Cantos*, though seldom at such
length) is an attitude of mind that is incompatible with the symbolist
poet's liberation of himself from the laws of time and space as those
operate in the observable world. In order to achieve that liberation the
poet had to forego any hope or conviction that the world outside himself was meaningful precisely insofar as it existed in its own right, something other than himself and bodied against him. There is all the difference in the world between identifying a swan with one's self, and
identifying one's self with a swan. It may be the difference between
Shelley's "Ode to a Skylark" (where the lark is important because it is
identified with Shelley) and a famous letter by Keats in which he identifies himself with a sparrow (where the sparrow is important because
Keats can identify himself with it, and so explore an order of being
other than his own.) Pound identifies himself with the baby wasp as

[5] Such reliance on the special Wordsworthian case tends to blunt the point of an
otherwise admirably penetrating essay by Peter Ure, "Yeats's 'Demon and
Beast'," in *Irish Writing* (Dublin, 1955), which makes very much the point about
Yeats that I have sought to make.

Keats with the sparrow. The wasp burrows into the earth to greet the chthonic powers of under-earth, just as Odysseus, in the *Odyssey* and time and again in the *Cantos*, must descend to the underworld to consult the Theban sage Tiresias. But at no point in the passage—not even if we remember how important for Pound, as for Lawrence, is such encountering of the chthonic powers of the loins and the libido—at no point does the wasp become a symbol for something in Pound's predicament, or for his ethical or other programs, or for his personality. The wasp retains its otherness as an independent form of life; it is only by doing so that it can be a source of comfort to the human observer:

> When the mind swings by a grass-blade
> an ant's forefoot shall save you

For, only if the ant is outside the human mind, can it, as we say, "take us out of ourselves" when we observe it and try to enter into its life. This quality of tenderness, and this capacity for sympathetic identification with inhuman forms of life, make up an attitude of reverent vigilance before the natural world, an attitude which, if it is no longer the attitude of the physicist, is still surely the habit of the biologist, in the field and the laboratory alike.

These are not the terms in which Pound is usually considered, partly because these are not the terms in which he talks of himself; nor is this lineage—Coleridge, Keats, Ruskin, Hopkins—the sort of family tree that Pound draws up for himself. Moreover, it is taken for granted that, if Pound has any claim on our attention at all, it is for what he has in common with Yeats and Eliot, not for that in him which distinguishes him from his old allies, whose names are so much more respectable. Yet it should be clear that if this sort of attention is not to be found in Yeats, it is unthinkable in Eliot, as in any man whose main interest in the external world is as a repertoire of objective correlatives for his own states of mind. "Old Possum's Book of Favourite Cats," for instance, is Eliot's one venture into light verse; and the assumption behind it, that cats cannot be taken seriously in poetry, seems arbitrary when set beside the seriousness on just this subject of Christopher Smart, for instance, or Baudelaire. Pound's cat, "Old Bulagaio's cat that with a well-timed leap/could turn the lever-shaped door handle" ("lever-shaped"—the exact observation anticipating the natural question, "how?") is more alive, more of a cat, than any of Eliot's.

Almost from the first, sure enough, Pound has defined his poetry as radically opposed to symbolist poetry. He confesses to having learned from Laforgue and from Corbière, still more from Rimbaud; but these poets he obviously does not regard as "symbolist." He claims to have learned much more from the non-symbolist Théophile Gautier than even from Rimbaud—a claim that J. J. Espey, in his book on *Hugh Selwyn Mauberley*, shows to be well founded. Pound puts it on record "que les poètes essentiels [as texts for English poets to study] se réduisent à Gautier, Corbière, Laforgue, Rimbaud. Que depuis Rimbaud, aucun poète en France n'a inventé rien de fondamental."[6] In 1918 he writes that "Mallarmé, perhaps unread, is apt to be slightly overestimated . . ."[7] and that "Imagisme is not symbolism. The symbolists dealt in 'association,' that is, in a sort of allusion, almost of allegory. They degraded the symbol to the status of a word. . . ." "Moreover," he says, writing in the period of the First World War, "one does not want to be called a symbolist, because symbolism has usually been associated with mushy technique." (*Gaudier-Brzeska*, p. 97)

Yeats and Pound were close and constant friends, and some of Pound's remarks on symbolism are beside the point because, like many people since, he takes Yeats as a typical symbolist; and this is far from the truth. In the Pisan Canto 83 there are two passages on Yeats. One of them, which follows almost immediately the page of sympathetic identification with the baby wasp, is Pound's hilarious account of the life at Stone Cottage, Coleman's Hatch, Sussex, where Yeats and Pound lived together at several periods between 1913 and 1916:

> There is fatigue deep as the grave.
> The Kakemono grows in flat land out of mist
>   sun rises lop-sided over the mountain
>   so that I recalled the noise in the chimney
> as it were the wind in the chimney
>
>   but was in reality Uncle William
> downstairs composing
> that had made a great Peeeeacock
>   in the proide ov his oiye
>   had made a great peeeeeeecock in the . . .
> made a great peacock
>   in the proide of his oyyee
>
>   proide ov his oy-ee
> as indeed he had, and perdurable

[6]*Letters*, p. 293 (letter to René Taupin, 1928).
[7]"French Poets," *The Little Review* (Feb. 1918); reprinted in *Make It New* (1934), p. 161.

        a great peacock aere perennius
            or as in the advice to the young man to
        breed and get married (or not)
                as you choose to regard it

        at Stone Cottage in Sussex by the waste moor
        (or whatever) and the holly bush
            who would not eat ham for dinner
        because peasants eat ham for dinner
            despite the excellent quality
        and the pleasure of having it hot

        well those days are gone forever
            and the travelling rug with the coon-skin tabs
        and his hearing nearly all Wordsworth
            for the sake of his conscience but
        preferring Ennemosor in Witches

        did we ever get to the end of Doughty:
            The Dawn in Britain?
                            perhaps not
          (Summons withdrawn, sir.)
        (bein' aliens in prohibited area)
        clouds lift their small mountains
            before the elder hills

The fineness of this is identical with the fineness of the passage on the wasp. The whole man, Yeats, is carried before us; we delight, as the poet has delighted, in his alien mode of being. His foibles, recorded with affectionate and amused indulgence—his way of *keening* rather than reading poetry, his "Gothick" interests ("preferring Ennemosor on Witches"), his preposterous snobbery ("because peasants eat ham for dinner")—do not in the least detract from, they only substantiate, the perception of his greatness. Out of this personality, with all its quirky eccentricities, comes something in the splendid Horatian phrase "aere perennius," more lasting than bronze, equal in its achieved conclusiveness to the metal singing-bird of Yeats's own "Byzantium" and to those sonnets by Shakespeare ("the advice to the young man to/breed and get married"), where Shakespeare himself makes the proud Horatian claim,

        Not marble, nor the gilded monuments
        Of princes, shall outlive this powerful rhyme;

It should be plain that this is very far indeed, in human terms, from Yeats's treatment of the Gregories, the Pollexfens, John O'Leary, Lionel Johnson, John Synge. It manifests a respect for the uniqueness and otherness of the other person, a flexibility of feeling incompatible with the Yeatsian private pantheon and his deliberately noble style, even in such a splendid poem as "The Municipal Gallery Revisited."

The other passage on Yeats in Canto 83 is shorter, but more immediately apposite, for it considers Yeats specifically as a symbolist, and at this point not unfairly:

> Le Paradis n'est pas artificiel
> and Uncle William dawdling around Notre Dame
> in search of whatever
>   paused to admire the symbol
> with Notre Dame standing inside it
> Whereas in St. Etienne
>   or why not Dei Miracoli:
> mermaids, that carving,
>
>   in the drenched tent there is quiet
>   sered eyes are at rest

"Le Paradis Artificiel" is the title of a book by Baudelaire about drugs and the beatific hallucinations they induce. Pound's rejection of the assumption behind it sounds as one of the strongest of many refrains that knit the later cantos together; it reappears, for instance, in an especially moving way in the Rock-Drill Canto 92. Pound's repeated assertion that the paradisal is *real*, out there in the real world, is a conscious challenge to the whole symbolist aesthetic. Hugh Kenner's gloss on this passage makes the essential point: "Yeats' incorrigibly symbologizing mind infected much of his verse with significance imposed on materials by an effort of will ('artificiel'). . . ."[8] Yeats can see Notre Dame as an artifact, a presence created in masonry and sculpture, only for the sake of what it answers to in him, not for what it is in itself. He must always arrange the perspective, and project upon the object the significance he can then read out of it. For Pound, to whom, ever since his friendship with Gaudier-Brzeska, cut and worked stone has been an especially fruitful source of presences and inscapes, this attitude is intolerable. Only when he sees stone in and for itself, the artist's working of it only a drawing out of what was latent in the stone to begin with—only then, as in the sculptures of S. Maria dei Miracoli in Venice, can it save him as the ant's forefoot could save him. Only by contemplating it thus can the "sered eyes" (both "seared" and "fallen into the sere, the yellow leaf") come to be "at rest."

[8]Hugh Kenner, *The Poetry of Ezra Pound* (London, 1951), p. 210.

M. L. Rosenthal

The Cantos

Space forbids our going into the *Cantos* in even as much detail as we have into *Mauberley*. We have already, however, noted some of the leading ideas behind this more involved and ambitious work, and though we cannot here trace their handling throughout its winding, Gargantuan progress, a few suggestions concerning its character as a poetic sequence may be useful. First of all, we may take as our point of departure the fact that in motivation and outlook the *Cantos* are a vast proliferation from the same conceptions which underlie *Mauberley*. The difference lies partly in the multiplicity of "voices" and "cross-sections," partly in the vastly greater inclusiveness of historical and cultural scope, and partly in the unique formal quality of the longer sequence; it is by the very nature of its growth over the years a work-in-progress. Even when the author at last brings it to conclusion, reorganizing it, supplying the withheld Cantos 72 and 73, completing his revisions, and even giving his book a definitive title, it will remain such a work. Each group of cantos will be what it is now—a new *phase* of the poem, like each of the annual rings of a living tree. The poet has put his whole creative effort into a mobilization of all levels of his consciousness into the service of the *Cantos*; there has been a driving central continuity, and around it new clusters of knowledge and association linked with the others by inter-weavings, repetitions, and over-all perspective. Pound has staked most of his adult career as a poet on this most daring of poetic enterprises; literary history gives us few other examples of comparable commitment.

From A Primer of Ezra Pound *(New York: Grosset and Dunlap, 1961). Copyright © 1961 by M. L. Rosenthal. Reprinted by permission of Macmillan Publishing Co. and New Directions Publishing Corporation.*

125

The *Cantos* has been called Pound's "intellectual diary since 1915," and so it is. But the materials of this diary have been so arranged as to subserve the aims of the poem itself. Passage by passage there *is* the fascination of listening in on a learned, passionate, now rowdy, now delicate intelligence, an intelligence peopled by the figures of living tradition but not so possessed by them that it cannot order their appearances and relationships. Beyond the fascination of the surface snatches of song, dialogue, and description, always stimulating and rhythmically suggestive though not always intelligible upon first reading, there is the essential overriding drive of the poem, and the large pattern of its overlapping layers of thought. The way in which the elements of this pattern swim into the reader's line of vision is well suggested by Hugh Kenner, one of Pound's most able and enthusiastic interpreters:

> The word "periplum," which recurs continually throughout the *Pisan Cantos* [74-84], is glossed in Canto LIX:
>
>> periplum, not as land looks on a map
>> but as sea bord seen by men sailing.
>
> Victor Brerard discovered that the geography of the *Odyssey*, grotesque when referred to a map, was minutely accurate according to the Phoenician voyagers' periploi. The image of successive discoveries breaking upon the consciousness of the voyager is one of Pound's central themes. . . . The voyage of Odysseus to hell is the matter of Canto I. The first half of Canto XL is a periplum through the financial press; "out of which things seeking an exit," we take up in the second half of the Canto the narrative of the Carthagenian Hanno's voyage of discovery. Atlantic flights in the same way raise the world of epileptic maggots in Canto XXVIII into a sphere of swift firm-hearted discovery. . . . The periplum, the voyage of discovery among facts, . . . is everywhere contrasted with the conventions and artificialities of the bird's eye view afforded by the map. . . .[1]

Thus, the successive cantos and layers of cantos must be viewed not so much schematically as experientially. Here we see how the early Pound's developing idealization of the concrete image, the precise phrase, the organically accurate rhythm are now brought to bear on this vast later task. The many voices, varied scenes and *personae*, and echoes of other languages and literatures than English reflect this emphasis on

[1] Hugh Kenner, *The Poetry of Ezra Pound* (Norfolk, Conn.: New Directions, 1951), pp. 102-103. Kenner's use of Roman numerals follows Pound, but the latest groups of cantos (*Rock-Drill* and *Thrones*), published after Kenner's book, change to Arabic numerals. For consistency's sake we have followed the latter usage throughout.

experience itself: something mysterious, untranslatable, the embodied meaning of life which we generalize only at peril of losing touch with it. So also with Pound's emphatic use of Chinese ideograms, whose picture-origins still are visible enough, he believes, so that to "read" them is to think in images rather than in abstractions. His use of them is accounted for by the same desire to present "successive discoveries breaking upon the consciousness of the voyager." The first effect of all these successive, varied breakings is not intended to be total intellectual understanding, any more than in real experience we "understand" situations upon first coming into them. But by and by the pattern shapes up and the relationships clarify themselves, though always there remains an unresolved residue of potentiality for change, intractable and baffling.

Pound's "voyager," upon whose consciousness the discoveries break, is, we have several times observed, a composite figure derived first of all from the poet-speaker's identification with Odysseus. A hero of myth and epic, he is yet very much of this world. He is both the result of creative imagination and its embodiment. He explores the worlds of the living, of the dead, and of the mythic beings of Hades and Paradise. Lover of mortal women as of female deities, he is like Zagreus a symbol of the life-bringing male force whose mission does not end even with his return to his homeland. Gradually he becomes all poets and all heroes who have somehow vigorously impregnated the culture. He undergoes (as do the female partners of his procreation and the *personae* and locales in time and space of the whole sequence) many metamorphoses. Hence the importance of the Ovidian metamorphosis involving the god Dionysus, the sea (the female element and symbol of change), and the intermingling of contemporary colloquial idiom and the high style of ancient poetry in Canto 2. The first canto had ended with a burst of praise for Aphrodite, goddess of love and beauty, and in language suggesting the multiple allusiveness of the sequence: to the Latin and Renaissance traditions, as well as the Grecian-Homeric, and to the cross-cultural implications suggested by the phrase "golden bough." The second canto takes us swiftly backward in the poetic tradition, and then to the classical poets and the Chinese tradition. All poets are one, as Helen and Eleanor of Aquitaine and Tyro (beloved of Poseidon) and all femininity are one and all heroes are one.

In the first two cantos, then, the "periplum" of the sequence emerges into view. Three main value-referents are established: a sexually and aesthetically creative world-view, in which artistic and mythical tradition provides the main axes; the worship of Bacchus-Dionysus-Zagreus as the best symbol of creativity in action; and the multiple hero—poet, voyager, prophet, observer, thinker. The next four *Cantos* expand the range of allusiveness, introducing for instance the figure of the Cid, a chivalric hero, to add his dimension to the voyager-protagonist's consciousness. Also, various tragic tales are brought to mind, extending the initial horror of Odysseus' vision of the dead and thus contributing to the larger scheme of the poet in the modern wasteland. In absolute contrast, pagan beatitudes are clearly projected in Canto 2 in the pictures of Poseidon and Tyro:

> Twisted arms of the sea-god,
> Lithe sinews of water, gripping her, cross-hold,
> And the blue-gray glass of the wave tents them . . .

and, at the scene's close, in the phallic "tower like a one-eyed great goose" craning up above the olive grove while the fauns are heard "chiding Proteus" and the frogs "singing against the fauns." This pagan ideal comes in again and again, sharp and stabbing against bleak backgrounds like the "petals on the wet, black bough" of the "Metro" poem. Thus, in Canto 3:

> Gods float in the azure air,
> Bright gods and Tuscan, back before dew was shed.

In Canto 4:

> Choros nympharum, goat-foot, with the pale foot alternate;
> Crescent of blue-shot waters, green-gold in the shallows,
> A black cock crows in the sea-foam . . .

In 4 and 5 both there are deliberate echoes of such poets as have a kindred vision (Catullus, Sappho, and others), set against the notes of evil and damnation. The lines from Sordello in 6 serve the same purpose:

> "Winter and Summer I sing of her grace,
> As the rose is fair, so fair is her face,
> Both Summer and Winter I sing of her,
> The snow makyth me to remember her."

The Lady of the troubadours, whose "grace" is a secularized transposition from that of Deity, is another manifestation of "the body of nymphs, and Diana" which Actaeon saw, as well as of what Catullus meant: "'Nuces!' praise, and Hymenaeus 'brings the girl to her man. . . .'"

After these archetypal and literary points of reference have been established, Cantos 8–19 move swiftly into a close-up of the origins of the modern world in the Renaissance, and of the victory of the anticreative over the active, humanistic values represented by Sigismundo Malatesta and a few others. (Canto 7 is transitional; in any case we can note only the larger groupings here.) The relation between the "Renaissance

Cantos" (8–11) and the "Hell Cantos" (14–16), with their scatological
picturings of the contemporary Inferno, is organic: the beginning and
the end of the same process of social corruption. The beautiful dialogue
on order in 13 provides a calm, contrasting center for this portion of
the sequence, and is supported by the paradisic glow and serenity of
Elysium, revealed in 16 and 17. The earlier cantos had given momentary
attention to Oriental poetry and myth and, as we have seen, Elysian
glimpses also. Now these motifs are expanded and related to a new context, bringing the sequence into revised focus but carrying all its earlier
associations along. This leaping, reshuffling, and reordering is the organ-
izational principle behind the growth, the "annual rings," of the *Cantos*.

The next ten cantos interweave the motifs of these first two groups
and prepare us for the next leap (in Cantos 30–41) of perspective. There
are various preparations for this leap, even as early as Canto 20, in which
there is a moment of comment from the "outside" as if to take stock
before hurtling onward. From their remote "shelf," "aerial, cut in the
aether," the disdainful lotus-eaters question all purposeful effort:

> "What gain with Odysseus,
> "They that died in the whirlpool
> "And after many vain labours,
> "Living by stolen meat, chained to the rowingbench,
> "That he should have a great fame
> "And lie by night with the goddess? . . ."

Is the question wisdom or cynicism? No matter. The poem, given the
human condition and the epic tasks that grow out of it, is held in check
but an instant before again plunging ahead. The *Cantos* accepts the
moral meaning and the moral responsibility of human consciousness.
The heroic ideal remains, as on the other hand the evil of our days remains even after the goddess' song against pity is heard at the beginning
of 30.

The new group (30–41) is, like the later Adams cantos (62–71), in
the main a vigorous attempt to present the fundamental social and economic principles of the Founding Fathers as identical with Pound's
own. Adams and Jefferson are his particular heroes, and there is an
effort to show that Mussolini's program is intended to carry these basic
principles, imbedded in the Constitution but perverted by banking interests, into action. Pound works letters and other documents, as well as
conversations real and imagined, into his blocks of verse, usually frag-
mentarily, and gives modern close-ups of business manipulations. The
method has the effect of a powerful exposé, particularly of the glimpsed
operations of munitions-profiteers. The cantos of the early 1930's have,
indeed, a direct connection with the interest in social and historical

documentation and rhetoric that marks much other work of the same period, and at the end of Canto 41 (in which Mussolini is seen) we should not be surprised to find an oratorical climax similar in effect to that of Poem IV in *Mauberley* (1919). As in the earlier groups, however, we are again given contrasting centers of value, especially in Canto 36 (which renders Cavalcanti's *A lady asks me*) and in Canto 39, whose sexually charged interpretation of the spell cast over Odysseus and his men on Circe's isle is one of Pound's purest successes.

The Chinese cantos (53-61) and the Pisan group (74-84) are the two most important remaining unified clusters within the larger scheme. Again, the practical idealism of Confucianism, like that of Jefferson and Adams, becomes an analogue for Pound's own ideas of order and of secular aestheticism. Canto 13 was a clear precursor, setting the poetic stage for this later extension. "Order" and "brotherly deference" are key words in Confucius' teachings; both princes and ordinary men must have order *within* them, each in his own way, if dominion and family alike are to thrive. These thoughts are not clichés as Pound presents them. We hear a colloquy that has passion, humor, and depth, and what our society would certainly consider unorthodoxy. Kung "said nothing of the 'life after death,'" he considered loyalty to family and friends a prior claim to that of the law, he showed no respect for the aged when they were ignorant through their own fault, and he advocated a return to the times "when the historians left blanks in their writings,/I mean for things they didn't know." The Chinese cantos view Chinese history in the light of these principles of ordered intelligence in action, with the ideogram *ching ming* (name things accurately) at the heart of the identity between Confucian and Poundian attitudes. "The great virtue of the Chinese language," writes Hugh Gordon Porteus, "inheres in its written characters, which so often contrive to suggest by their graphic gestures (as English does by its phonetic gestures) the very essence of what is to be conveyed."[2] The development of Pound's interest in Chinese poetry and thought, as well as his varied translations from the Chinese, is in itself an important subject. This interest, like every other to which he has seriously turned his attention, he has brought directly to bear on his own poetic practice and on his highly activistic thinking in general.

With the *Pisan Cantos* and *Rock-Drill*[3] we are brought, first, into the immediately contemporary world of the poet himself, in Fascist

[2] "Ezra Pound and the Chinese Character: A Radical Examination," in *Ezra Pound*, p. 215.

[3] *Section: Rock-Drill: 85-95 de los cantares* (New York: New Directions, 1956). This was the first group of *Cantos* to be published separately since the *Cantos* appeared in 1948.

Italy toward the close of World War II, in a concentration camp at Pisa, during the last days of Mussolini; and second, into a great, summarizing recapitulation of root-attitudes developed in all the preceding cantos: in particular the view of the banking system as a scavenger and breeder of corruption, and of ancient Chinese history as an illuminating, often wholesomely contrasting analogue to that of the post-medieval West. Even more than before, we see now how the *Cantos* descend, with some bastardies along the line, from the Enlightenment. They conceive of a world creatively ordered to serve human needs, a largely rationalist conception. Hence the stress on the sanity of Chinese thought, the immediacy of the Chinese ideogram, and the hardheaded realism of a certain strain of economic theory. The *Pisan Cantos* show Pound's vivid responsiveness as he approached and passed his sixtieth birthday: his aliveness to people, his Rabelaisian humor, his compassion. The Lotus-Eaters of Canto 20, aloof and disdainful, have missed out on the main chances. Canto 81 contains the famous "Pull down thy vanity" passage in which the poet, though rebuking his own egotism, yet staunchly insists on the meaningfulness of his accomplishment and ideals. As the sequence approaches conclusion, the fragments are shored together for the moral summing-up. In the *Rock-Drill* section, Cantos 85-95, the stocktaking continues and we are promised, particularly in Canto 90, an even fuller revelation than has yet been vouchsafed us of the Earthly Paradise.

Cantos 96-109[4] begin to carry out this promise, though after so many complexities, overlappings, and interlocking voices it must be nearly impossible to bring the work to an end. It is essentially a self-renewing process rather than a classical structure, and there is no limit to the aspects of history and thought the poet has wished to bring to bear on the poem. Canto 96, for instance, touches on certain developments after the fall of Rome, especially two decrees in the Eastern Empire by Justinian and Leo VI concerning standards of trade, workmanship, and coinage. The special emphasis in this canto on Byzantine civilization is particularly appropriate because of Byzantium's historical and geographical uniting of East and West as well as its mystical associations pointing to a new and dramatic paradisic vision. Although the memory of earlier glimpses of "paradise" and the recapitulative, self-interrupting method militate against an effect of a revelation overwhelmingly new, the pacing of the whole sequence has made this difficulty at the end inevitable. Pound's conclusion must be introduced as emergent from the midst of things, still struggling from all in life and consciousness that makes for disorder.

[4] *Thrones: 96-109 de los cantares* (New York: New Directions, 1959).

Richard Pevear

Notes on the Cantos *of Ezra Pound*

> *It is all one to me where I begin; for I shall come back there again in time.* —Parmenides

I

The latest volume of the Cantos *(Drafts and Fragments of Cantos CX-CXVII)* appeared in 1969, over fifty years after the poem was begun. In the meantime, many of Pound's most faithful readers have died, and many critics have lost heart. It has been easier to assume that the poem is not going anywhere than to wait for it to get there. And yet that is an error. Pound has lived through the composition of the *Cantos*; he has given the years of his maturity and of his old age to the poem, and this length of time has not been simply a mechanical succession of hours and years during which the work was done but a period of personalized, organic time, bound up with the existence of the poet. That period is coming to an end. The latest cantos are not a continuation of an endless, shapeless poem, nor are they a trailing off of inspiration and an admission of failure, though they might give reason to think so. They are the ordained end of the poem, towards which Pound has been working from the start. What they reveal was implicit in the poem all the time, but Pound had to live through everything in order to reach that end.

"Notes on the Cantos of Ezra Pound," by Richard Pevear. From The Hudson Review, XXV, 1 (Spring, 1972), 51-70. Reprinted by permission of the author and The Hudson Review.

There is a feeling of wholeness in the *Cantos* that is very hard to explain. It may be, in part, that Pound's work represents a wide range of modulations of a single voice. But it is more than that. The difficulty of explanation comes, I think, from Pound's particular attentiveness to the existence (as opposed to the meaning) of poetry. What I mean by the existence of poetry can be partially explained by the way the image, as Pound has defined it, communicates: as opposed to the abstract statement, the image, like the metaphor, constantly recreates its perception. A fragment of narrative can work in the same way. It presents something, but what does it mean? Poetry can vary widely between the two poles of existence and meaning; Pound's work clearly tends towards image and embodiment.

In Canto CXVI there are two passages that contain a recognition that is central to the question of the poem's unity. First:

> And I am not a demigod,
> I cannot make it cohere.

And then:

> to "see again"
> the verb is "see," not "walk on"
> i.e. it coheres all right
>   even if my notes do not cohere.

The first passage reflects back on the whole of the poem and reveals it as incoherent, a ruin. The second passage qualifies the first; here Pound reaffirms the poem, but seen in a new way. It is not immediately clear what he means in either passage. Pound's detractors would be quick to agree that the poem does not cohere; they have been saying nothing else for years. But the second passage asserts a different kind of coherence, the very wholeness, I think, that I find so hard to explain. The two passages are not really contradictory, and in order to see the unity of the *Cantos* we must accept both of them.

These three observations are my starting point: that the growth of the poem is closely bound up with the existence of the poet in time; that the poem is hard to "read" because of Pound's attentiveness to the existence of poetry in image and embodiment; and that these "notes" which are the *Cantos* stand in relation to the coherence of their vision as an image stands to the insight it embodies.

Pound's poetry has its source in "the noblest of the senses," the eyes. But for Pound, seeing is rich in implications: eyesight leads to

insight, and clarity of perception is the basis for ethical life. He gives
us the paradigm of these connections in Canto LXXXI:

> First came the seen, then thus the palpable
>   Elysium, though it were in the halls of hell.

Pound's intelligence is visual in its most fundamental instincts. Hence
his theories of the image and the ideogram as forms of poetic expression, and the frequent analogy to sculpture in his writings about poetry.
Sculpture has precisely the qualities Pound considers highest in art:
solidity and clarity of embodiment. In sculpture, inward vision stands
in the light. And in the imagery of the *Cantos*, nature is embodied in
the light of the sun. Even in the smallest perceptions, it is the play of
light that draws Pound's eye:

> The water-bug's mittens show on the bright rock
>   below him.

To the Greeks, the light of the sun was the giver of true vision. The
Greek word for truth, *aletheia*, means unveiling. In a lecture delivered
in Munich in 1953, Heidegger spoke of the relationship in Greek art
between *techne* (skill or production) and *aletheia*:

> Why did [art] bear the humble name of *techne*? Because it was a
> pro-ductive unveiling and was thus a form of *poiesis*. The name
> *poiesis* was finally given, as its proper name, to the unveiling which
> penetrates and rules all the art of the beautiful: poetry, the poetic
> object. . . .
>   Poetry places truth in the shining-light of what Plato, in the
> *Phaedrus*, calls *to ekphanestaton*, that which resplends in the most
> pure way.

Poetry springs from the union of *techne* and *aletheia*, skill and revelation: from a moment of genesis in which light is both active and reserved, the light that penetrates into the truth of being, and the light
that in its shining makes vision possible. Pound is a poet, not a thinker,
but he suggests by brief quotations the thought that accompanies his
poetic making. For instance, one line from the remains of Erigena's
writings recurs in several of the later cantos: *Omnia quae sunt lumina
sunt/* All things that are are lights.

> in the light of light is the virtù
>   "sunt lumina" said Erigena Scotus.
>   (Canto LXXIV)

And in Canto XC, the fragment: *Ubi amor ibi oculus est*, identifies light with love "which proceeds from the soul." *Amor*, the inner potency of light, desires no more than an abiding union with the light of the sun, it changes nothing. Erotic passion, on the other hand, is blind.

The realm of light in the *Cantos* is the natural world, the physical present. But not the momentary present that is continually being thrust into the past. It is a timeless moment, the mystical *nunc stans*, in which the present, become transparent, is one with the "sun-warmed earth" of Odysseus' homecoming, the well-ordered kingdom of Confucius, the earthly paradise Virgil describes to Dante in the *Purgatorio*:

> *Vedi lo sol che in fronte ti riluce;*
> *vedi l'erbetta, i fiori e li arbuscelli*
> *che qui la terra sol da sè produce.*[1]
> (XXVII, 133-135)

But set against this self-born, light-filled world, obscuring it, allowing it to appear only in flashes, is the world of history. History is darkness in the *Cantos*, an underworld, a swamp, an ooze, a chaos. Caught in the flood of time, human actions are drawn back, down, away from the light. History is Lethe, the river of forgetfulness, concealment. It is here that Pound locates the dramatic episodes of the poem. The unifying action of the *Cantos* is the struggle to move from the darkness of history into the light of the sun.

This is not exactly a religious vision, at least it is of no known religion, though it has affinities with many. The greatest poetry of light is in the *Paradiso*. Pound has always been aware of the religious nature of poetry, but because of his love for clarity of form and perception, he has always detested religious humbug. He swept it aside as part of the Victorian confusion, which it was. Essentially, Pound distrusts the vagueness of spirituality. He loves good workmanship, and would prefer a blasphemous poem if it were well written over a pious poem whose only recommendation was its piety. His master, Dante, was a great poetic craftsman. He was also a religious visionary. Dante's skill as a poet can be admired in isolation, but in truth it cannot be separated from his religious vision. Dante's spiritual experience led him to clear eyesight. Pound, born in a time of spiritual forgetting and con-

---

[1] See there the sun that shines upon thy brow;
   See the young grass, the flowers and coppices
  Which this soil, of itself alone, makes grow.

                                                      (Binyon translation)

fusion, came back to clear eyesight and the physical world. And yet
Dante remained his master in poetry.

Pound turned from the spiritual world to history. In this he is the
product of his time. Historical determinism has long been the prevail-
ing, the outward and established, basis of thought and social theory,
despite the conflicts among its various ideologies. But Pound is a poet,
not an ideologist, and while he has been caught up in the conflicts of
this century and has suffered greatly for his errors, he has persisted in
living through these experiences without betraying the demands of his
art. In the end, he is able to summarize his vision of history in two
short lines that speak for depths of experience:

> The hells move in cycles,
>   No man can see his own end.
>   (Canto CXIII)

There could be no more concise and forceful expression of the in-
completeness of the historical world, of the absence of spirit and the
absence of a sense of personal destiny which turn history into hell.

Pound is left with the cycles of hells. And he is left with the
changes of nature, which he captures still in images of great beauty
but with more understanding in the last cantos:

> . . . to think what has been shall be.
>   flowing, ever unstill.
>
> Then a partridge-shaped cloud over duststorm.
>   (Canto CXIII)

Yet he does not deify either nature or history, and in that refusal lies
much of his greatness. We may realize, reading the *Cantos*, that for
several centuries men have been trying to see transcendent purposes or
an eschatological meaning in the forces of history or nature, and have
thus blinded themselves to both the spirit and the flesh. The *Cantos*
are not a celebration of forces, but of light.

Pound was unaware of, or else indifferent to, the most intimate
struggle of our time, a current of spiritual rebellion against the prevail-
ing historicism: the work of the Russian novelists, of Russian thinkers
like Shestov and Berdyaev, of Kierkegaard, Unamuno, and Simone
Weil, of Franz Kafka and Antonio Machado. Some of these writers
have appeared only recently or posthumously; others lived on the
periphery of Europe. All of them are more or less disquieted beings,

paradoxical and self-contradictory. They are digging for treasure in the darkest regions of existence, and nothing is clear or of firm outline in their work except the clear, hard light of their spirituality. And all of them have this in common: they cannot resign themselves to the hells of history and the closed cycles of nature. Pound's vision is related to theirs, but they are standing back to back: he looks precisely where they find nothing to see.

The *Cantos* carry into the open, into recognition, the ruin of history. A distinction should be made between the world of the epic and the worlds of fiction. The epic is always rooted in historical experience; it bears a high degree of fleshly suffering, and only a small degree of imagination or fantasy. The fiction of spiritual rebellion in our time has created many fantastic worlds. But Pound has rediscovered and opened up the epic world. In holding open the image of the ruin of history, without falling into a deification of force, he achieves the lucidity of epic vision. In a *propos* on the epic, the French thinker Alain has written:

> All pious deceptions are foreign to the epic. A just and good God, as in the *Jerusalem*, is no god of armies. No, it is the caprice of the gods that represents so well the play of blind forces. After courage, flight; after the force that knows no self-doubt, the fatigue that doubts everything. The gods dispense the one and the other, as they throw down rain, storm, lightning. And man is so made that these bitter reflections do not turn him from combat; on the contrary he gives himself up to his own forces, storm against storm. At the same time, the wise laws, the prudent life, the kinds of work whose end is the conservation of life, these are pure memories from which man finds himself forever separated. It is thus that he is able to see them.

In the *Iliad*, the "other" world, the world of natural harmony and peace, appears only in the similes, in glimpses, as a lost world. The epic stands astonished for a moment, then the madness breaks in again. There are similar moments in the *Cantos:*

> Sun up; work
> sundown; to rest
> dig well and drink of the water
> dig field, eat of the grain
> Imperial power is? and to us what is it?
>
> The fourth; the dimension of stillness.
> And the power over wild beasts.
> (Canto XLIX)

We come upon such passages and we wonder at the intensity of emotion Pound creates with them. How else should we understand this, how else understand, for example, the presence of Confucius and the teachings of Confucius throughout the poem, but as glimpses of a possible world which we are able to see because we are forever separated from it? Pound is not preaching Confucianism. He is not preaching against usury in the usury cantos. He offers no critique of any kind. The verb is "to see."

If we take Dante's poem as the model of coherent vision, neither the *Iliad*, nor the *Cantos*, nor the works of the "treasure diggers" are coherent. They are all rooted in existence. Dante's vision came to him from the beyond.

Pound returns to the sources of epic poetry, but his poem is in no way a copy of the ancient epic. Homer makes use of the devices of oral poetry, and many writers of literary epics have studiously copied him. Pound, on the other hand, makes use of the devices of print, not only in the layout of the page, but in his basic technique of the suppression of narrative links, which presupposes a fixed text. And there are more important differences. The *Iliad* is the tragedy of men delivered up to force; the Homeric cosmos is a severe order ruled by Fate, unconcerned with human suffering and deaf to supplications; the great opponent to the individual will of man is the dispensation of the universe. In the *Cantos*, the great opponent is history. It was Berdyaev who said, "there is a tragic conflict between history, with its complex movements and agencies, and man, with his unique and irreducible personal destiny." Finally, Pound does not share Homer's objectivity. He is implicated in the poem as he is in the act of writing it. The latest cantos reveal his implication, but at the same time they project the image of the poet beyond personal failure:

> I have brought the great ball of crystal;
>   who can lift it?
> Can you enter the great acorn of light?
>   But the beauty is not the madness
> Tho' my errors and wrecks lie about me.
>   (Canto CXVI)

The action of the *Cantos* is the making of the poem, and the protagonist is the poet.

II

> *When Socrates believed that there was a God,*
> *he saw very well that where the way swings off*
> *there is also an objective way of approximation,*
> *for example by the contemplation of nature*
> *and human history, and so forth. His merit*
> *was precisely to shun this way, where the*
> *quantitative siren song enchants the mind and*
> *deceives the existing individual.—Kierkegaard,*
> *Concluding Unscientific Postscript*

The *Cantos* are a poem containing history. That idea was Pound's starting point, the intuition that led him to engage in the act of creating the poem, and as a beginning it is both clear and ambiguous: it is clear in delimiting the realm of the poem but it does not define any particular structure or end. Since Aristotle, poetry and history have been considered separate realms. The historian Burckhardt accepted Aristotle's judgment that poetry is superior to history, "because the faculty that gives birth to poetry is intrinsically higher than that of the greatest historian." What, then, is a poem containing history? How can a poet take history into his poem without either lowering poetry or making history transcendent? Does poetry become historical, or does history become poetic, in a poem containing history?

Canto I is narrated almost to the end by Odysseus and is largely a translation of the *Odyssey*, book 11. But it is not a translation of Homer. It is a translation into English alliterative verse of a Latin translation of Homer made by Andreas Divus in 1538. And it is not entirely a translation. When Odysseus meets Tiresias in the underworld, the prophet asks him:

> A second time? why? man of ill star
> Facing the sunless dead and this joyless region?

Here Odysseus becomes not only Homer's hero but also the first and ruling character of the *Cantos*, forced to return a second time to the region of the dead to receive the prophecy of his homecoming. The whole of the poem grows out of this first gesture of the return into Hades, which Pound endows with a rich simultaneity of meaning. He is not interested in recreating the character of Odysseus and fitting him out with new adventures. His Odysseus is the Odysseus of Homer, who reappeared during the Renaissance in Divus's version. The character is mythological, but the poem is real. Pound gives us the date: 1538. This is a historical point of view.

In the next canto a parallel distinction is made:

> Hang it all, Robert Browning,
> there can be but the one "Sordello."
> But Sordello, and my Sordello?
> Lo Sordels si fo di Mantovana.

The lines are simply an orientation; in them, Pound throws off the trappings of fiction. Browning took the name Sordello and created poetic fiction around it. Pound gives us a single line, a fragment in Provençal referring to the real Sordello. Historically, there is only one Sordello. The quotations from foreign languages, like the passages of translation, are placed in the *Cantos* because they are historical facts. An idea in its original expression, a remnant of poetry, are historical facts of the first order, provided their original form is respected. Pound is not interested in writing a sequel to the *Odyssey* or his own "Sordello." He is interested in the appearance at a certain point in history of a translation of Homer or of a particular poet. He lets these facts speak; or better, he draws out of memory their original voices.

The first two cantos reveal Pound's practice, and thereby something of his vision, throughout the poem. We can make one necessary and surprising observation: there is nothing fictional, nothing mythological, nothing allegorical in the *Cantos.* Poetry in Pound's hands is an instrument of perception, not the medium of imagination. The myths that appear and reappear in the *Cantos* stand as historical evidence; that is, Pound does not retell ancient stories, he recalls them, as embodiments of a certain force of spirit or transcending will which may rightly be called historical because it led to the building of temples, the carving of stone, the ordering of the calendar. It is the reserved power of myths, a power unknown to fiction, that Pound recalls. The *Cantos* are a poem containing history. Whatever is not history in them is drawn from nature.

But history usually implies sequence, and sequence implies an idea or theory of history through which the separate historical facts are drawn together and interpreted as a whole, a fabric or a process. The *Cantos,* on the contrary, are a collection of fragments that do not form a whole sequence. Renaissance history is interrupted by American history, which is interrupted by Chinese history, and they are all interrupted by topical references and natural images. We read about Italian banking, we read parts of a letter of Jefferson on the Erie Canal project, we read parts of Confucian classics. Never do we get a coherent picture of the sequence of history, even of the sequence of one man's thoughts or acts. If this is a poem containing history, it is unintelligible from a historical point of view.

We come back to the question of poetry and history: if a historian looks for sequence or wholeness, what does a poet look for? Jacob Burckhardt called history the record of active humanity. Poetry is related to activity only "archetypally." That is, a poet may portray a man of action like Achilles, but he is not concerned with the details of the life of a man like Julius Caesar. Poetry is drawn to great *actions,* to single gestures, for all that is in them; it is not drawn to the business of marking out and running an empire. Historians present activity as a continuum of actions. Interruption of the continuum creates gestures. (In his essay, "What is Epic Theater?" Walter Benjamin has noted: ". . . the more frequently someone is interrupted in the act of acting, the more gestures result.") Interruption projects the moment out of time, just as quotation tears a fragment from its context and holds it up to a new light. For all such interruptions, death is the great model. To the historian, death has a relative position in the unending flow of events. But for living men, death is an absolute calamity, an event of a higher order, a moment which throws the whole of existence back into question. It is by allegiance to the sovereignty of death that poetry rises above history. Poetry recognizes that moments speak more than sequences, that in a moment the whole of a man's life—body, energy, spirit—can be revealed; whereas in order to see sequence you must limit your view to a single area of activity, and to see the whole fabric of a period is to lose sight of the living man. Pound embodies history through poetic vision. To demand historical sequence or wholeness from the *Cantos* is to mistake poetry for history.

Pound finds many translucent moments in history, and these moments become a kind of destiny for the man, just as the shades in Hades are held eternally in the attitudes of their deaths, at the moment when destiny touched them. Elpenor remains in our minds, caught in a single line: "a man of no fortune, and with a name to come." Confucius stands against an eternal background in the words Pound gives him:

> The blossoms of the apricot
> blow from the east to the west,
> And I have tried to keep them from falling.
>   (Canto XIII)

Pound does not use historical figures to "stand for" general human types or to exemplify human qualities. They are who they are; when they speak, it is often in words from their own writings or from contemporary records. Just as the nature imagery in the *Cantos* is not placed in the poem for atmosphere and serves no metaphorical purpose, but is an embodiment of the shining presence of the world.

Implicit in Pound's concern with existence and in his search for moments, is a third fact of great importance for understanding the *Cantos* as a whole. Narrative usually implies the unfolding of events in time, but while the *Cantos* have the appearance of a narrative poem and contain many fragments of narrative, the movement of the poem from beginning to end is not a temporal but a spatial unfolding, the completion of a single, manifold vision which is essentially static. The completion of the vision takes time, in the writing or in the reading, but the time it takes is not active in the poem. This paradox appears whenever human destiny is in question. However, to say that the vision of the poem is static is not to say that Pound's poetry is objectivized and generic or that he performs the superb trick of negating time. By the very nature of his concern with history, Pound finds the emotion of time at the heart of the poem—the emotion of time lost, of time wasted, of the pastness or the passing away of time, of time unredeemed. But the emotion of time is itself timeless. History in the *Cantos* is not an ongoing process, but a condition.

The *Cantos* begin with a return to the Homeric underworld, which is the world of history, seen poetically, as it is in Homer. And the poem never leaves the hell of history, even at the end. Those who apply to the *Cantos* Pound's occasional suggestion that he might follow the structure of Dante's poem have tried to see the later cantos as a *Paradiso.* But they are not a *Paradiso.* Dante's poem is a comedy, but the *Cantos* are tragic. History becomes transcendent and symbolic in the Christian cosmos; lacking mercy, history takes on flesh and blood. But in the *Cantos* we are aware, as we could not be in Homer, of the absence of paradise, aware that the vision of paradise has vanished or has been lost. And thus Tiresias's question gains its full meaning:

A second time? why? man of ill star
Facing the sunless dead and this joyless region?

Daniel Pearlman

Canto 1 as Microcosm

Through the symbolic use of Greek myth, the first canto suggests not only the major themes to be elaborated in the poem, but foreshadows, like a microcosm, the total structural development of the *Cantos*. Except for the last seven lines, Canto 1 consists of Pound's abbreviated English translation of Andreas Divus's Renaissance Latin translation of the opening lines of the eleventh book of the *Odyssey*. Book XI is called the "Book of the Dead" or "Nekuia," because it concerns Odysseus' visit to Hades.[1] The blood-sacrifice Odysseus makes to Tiresias, who gives the voyager prophetic counsel on how to return to Ithaca, announces the *Cantos'* all-embracing theme of the need for cultural renewal—man's need to reestablish contact with whatever has been vital in his cultural heritage so that he may know what meaningful course to pursue in the future.

Pound begins his epic in the midst of chronological or narrative time, *in medias res*. But in another and deeper sense he begins outside this

[1] E. M. Glenn, *The Analyst*, No. VIII (Department of English, Northwestern University, n.d.), p.3. (*The Analyst,* in mimeographed form, appears irregularly under the general editorship of Robert Mayo. The intention of the publication with regard to the *Cantos* has been mainly to provide scholarly background rather than critical interpretation.) My own debt to *The Analyst* is considerable, for it is one of the chief scholarly sources for the first eleven cantos.

"profane" flow of time, for the Nekuia and the ritual act of sacrifice abolish chronological time and place Odysseus in the timeless realm of unchanging myth. The historical chain of events, the concatenation of cause and effect, is broken and will no longer determine the fate of Pound's Odysseus until such time as he disregards Tiresias' wisdom and deviates from the pattern of behavior prescribed by the myth. Just as Odysseus' act of blood-sacrifice puts him in touch with the living past and contradicts the irreversible flow of historical time, so too Pound's reverent act of *translation* denies meaning to historical time by showing Homer still to be alive in the so-called present. This translation of a translation of Homer collapses time and makes coeval not three, but actually five different layers of civilization. Not only is there a continuity of creative impulse between Homeric Greece, Renaissance Italy, and the present, but the Anglo-Saxon rhythms of Pound's English suggest another period whose vital spark has been recaptured; and the Renaissance Latin of Andreas Divus evidences the living continuity of the classical Latin tongue as a literary vehicle.

In the original version of the present canto, then entitled "Canto III," Divus's translation is introduced by the following comment, which quotes Burckhardt: "More than the Roman city, the Roman speech"/ (Holds fast its part among the ever-living)." Pound wants us to understand especially that Divus has dealt fittingly with Homer, has "Caught up his cadence, word and syllable."[2] When Pound, in line 68 of Canto 1 as it now stands, says, "Lie quiet Divus," this is indeed a critical moment in the canto, but the command is not as cryptic as *The Analyst* would suppose. It is simply that Pound has propitiated Divus's ghost by the sacrificial offering of vital translation, just as Odysseus has satisfied Tiresias' ghost by giving it new life through a blood transfusion. In the same way, Divus might have said, "Lie quiet Homer," after successfully translating him into Latin. Whatever was truly alive in the past, Pound is saying through all this, is always capable of rebirth; and the dead weight of historical time can always be abolished.

There is no conscious intimation here of the theme of organic time, which Pound will set in opposition to mechanical time in the middle phase of the *Cantos*. And yet the Nekuia of Canto 1, which suggests the need to renew vital contact with the cultural tradition, stands as prototype for the later Nekuia passage of Canto 47, which mythically represents man's need for vital contact with chthonic nature and the cosmic and seasonal cycles, a contact which must serve as the basis of cultural renewal. The myths, symbols, and structure of Canto 1 foreshadow the major developments of theme and structure in the poem as a whole.

Time in the first canto is Odysseus' antagonist. It is broadly sym-

[2] Ezra Pound, "Canto III," *Poetry X* (August 1917), p. 250.

bolized by the rough, inimical sea, "spiteful Neptune," as Tiresias calls it, which Odysseus will overcome but at the loss of "all companions." It is historical time which Pound's Odysseus must conquer, and the souls of its victims rise up "out of Erebus"—"souls stained with recent tears," men "mauled with bronze lance heads"—crowding about Odysseus and crying out to him and to Pound for more blood sacrifices, which I read as a symbolic cry for vindication against the brutality of history. The sea symbolizes not only history, but even more obviously nature, both of which the will must learn to cope with if it is creatively to transform the environment. And Odysseus *polumetis,* the man of many counsels or wiles, dramatizes the creative will capable of effective resistance to the destructive countercurrents of historical time.

The Odyssean voyager-poet of the *Cantos* stands in marked contrast to the Odyssean poet-hero of the *Hugh Selwyn Mauberley* sequences, which Pound wrote while putting the finishing touches on the early cantos. Mauberley is a type of the ineffectual aesthete of the 'Nineties. In the first poem of the sequence, which sums up his failure to make an impression on his environment, Mauberley is presented as an Odysseus "out of key with his time" who has "Observed the elegance of Circe's hair" without having gained the wisdom needed to bridge the gap between his poetic self and the world. The result, in the second sequence, is Pound's vision of a Mauberley seen passively *drifting,* not actively steering, in the suspiciously calm waters of an utterly psychotic withdrawal from reality. Announcing his end, he writes on an oar "Here drifted/an hedonist,"[3] and the suggestion is of the fate of drunken Elpenor in the *Odyssey* and in Pound's first canto. *Mauberley* depicts the downhill journey of a comparatively narrow, will-less aesthete, quite unlike the Odysseus of Canto 1, who is heroically many-minded and active in gaining wisdom for the effective exertion of his will upon the environment.

If *Mauberley* presents Pound's conception of the poet as decadent, the *Cantos* presents Pound's conception of the poet as hero, whose ideal role is actively to exert a determining influence on the social environment. Odysseus is the archetype for all those later "heroes" of active, creative will who crop up in the *Cantos:* Malatesta, Confucius, Thomas Jefferson, Mussolini, and others. Odysseus against the sea, the initial image of the poem, establishes in symbolic form the basic polarity or conflict of forces which will reappear in many guises throughout the *Cantos* but can always be reduced to the formulation of will versus nature or will versus history. The polarity which I have suggested earlier to be all-encompassing remains that of *spirit* and *time* (for the concept of time ultimately includes both nature and history).

[3]*Personae* (New York, 1950), p. 203.

The second part of Canto 1, consisting of the last seven lines only, is a flash preview of the spiritual adventures in store for the poet-hero of the *Cantos*. As opposed to the rational narrative style of the Nekuia passage, the method here is elliptical, discontinuous, and the tone is oracular or *prophetic,* for reasons which I will soon make clear. The brevity of the passage makes it worth quoting in full:

> And he sailed, by Sirens and thence outward and away
> And unto Circe
>   Venerandam,
> In the Cretan's phrase, with the golden crown, Aphrodite,
> Cypri munimenta sortita est, mirthful, oricalchi, with golden
> Girdles and breast bands, thou with dark eyelids
> Bearing the golden bough of Argicida. So that:

The first two lines reverse the actual sequence of events in Book XII of the *Odyssey*, where, after leaving the underworld, Odysseus first re-joins Circe and later encounters the Sirens. The apparent justification for the reversal is that Pound is presenting images of the feminine in ascending order of desirability. We shall meet the Sirens, Circe, and Aphrodite later on, always in significant contexts, throughout the *Cantos*. First mentioned in the passage quoted are the Sirens, whose beauty promises only disaster. The ambiguous Circe is next, the goddess who can turn men to swine or, if dominated by Odysseus, provide phy-sical love and practical guidance. Aphrodite is the "crown" of feminine beauty, and because she is "venerandam," worthy of reverence, she symbolizes equally the spiritual dimensions of such beauty.

The same sea of nature, the same life-force, throws up these three possibilities of experience for Odysseus, which range from physical danger to the most exalted vision of beauty. It is worth noting that Pound, unlike T. S. Eliot, rejects dualism and does not regard material and spiritual reality as essentially at odds. In an early essay he speaks favorably of Remy de Gourmont, who "does not grant the duality of body and soul, or at least suggests that this medieval duality is unsatis-factory; there is an interpenetration, an osmosis of body and soul, at least for hypothesis."[4] Pound goes on to praise Gourmont's "concep-tion of love, passion, emotion as an intellectual instigation," and throughout the *Cantos* we shall see that Aphrodite, goddess of love, stands for both physical passion and for the highest and most enduring kind of beauty that the spirit of man motivated by love can create. In

[4]Ezra Pound, "Remy de Gourmont," in *Literary Essays*, ed. T. S. Eliot (Norfolk, 1954), p. 341.

one way or another all the villains of the poem attempt to deny, repress, or abuse sex, nature, the life-force in any and all of its forms; the heroes try to enter into creative harmony with nature.

Pound's non-dualistic view of nature as a physical-spiritual continuum is so important to the *Cantos* that it is worth giving it a name. I find the term *holism,* as defined by Jan Smuts in *Holism and Evolution,* the most fitting one available. Holism, says Smuts,

> represents the organic order as arising from and inside the inorganic or physical order without in any way derogating from it. If in the end it erects on the physical a superstructure which is more and more ideal and spiritual, that does not mean a denial of the physical. The idealism of Holism does not deny matter, but affirms and welcomes and affectionately embraces it.[5]

The pagan, and the archaic man in general, have tended to regard the world holistically, at least in the sense of a physical-spiritual continuum. Odysseus' communication with Tiresias through the blood of a sacrificed sheep symbolizes, in Canto 1, Pound's belief that the world of spirit and the world of nature are interdependent aspects of the same underlying *Ding an sich* that manifests itself temporally in the form of polarity. One of the most important metaphysical principles of Confucianism, the philosophy which informs the *Cantos* from beginning to end (as we shall see), is just this holistic principle expressed by the sage and rendered thus in Pound's translation:

> The celestial and earthly process can be defined in a single phrase; its actions and its creations have no duality.[6]

When the last seven lines of Canto 1 are examined in the light of the holistic principle, Aphrodite and the Sirens are seen as the two polar extremes of the *Ding an sich* which is nature. Circe, as a mediating center between the destructive and creative extremes, will come to represent that harmony with nature which Odysseus-Pound must attain before he can be vouchsafed the vision of Aphrodite. The point is that nature will be for man no more than what he wills it to be, its creative or destructive effects on him depending entirely on the quality of his will

[5] Jan Christiaan Smuts, *Holism and Evolution* (New York, 1961), p. 329. (Originally published in 1926.) I might mention here that Pound has told me he did not read Smuts.
[6] Ezra Pound, trans., *Confucius*: The Great Digest & Unwobbling Pivot (New York, 1951), p. 183.

—or, better, the direction of his will. This concept of the direction of the will is the foundation of Pound's ethical world-view. Whether it be the creation of an enduring work of art or of a lasting social order, neither comes about by chance. It is "a matter of Will," says Pound. "It is also a matter of the Direction of the Will," and "this phrase," he says, "brings us ultimately both to Confucius and Dante."[7] It was in Dante's *De vulgari eloquentia* "that Pound . . . discovered the term *directio voluntatis,* link between Confucius and the best of medieval Europe."[8] Pound takes the Confucian ideogram 志 as "The will, the direction of the will, . . . the officer standing over the heart."[9] The ideogram can thus represent the harmonious conjunction of Odysseus and the sea, the will and nature, or Kung (Confucius) and Eleusis. In the *Cantos* Kung stands for the principle of order, the force of reason, intelligence, and human-heartedness, whereas Eleusis stands for Dionysian energy, the life-force itself. Civilizations rise because of Eleusinian energy, but they are maintained in health and stability by Kung, the principle of order.

If the proper direction of the will is the result of an educative process, then it seems to me clear that the three necessary stages in the development of the will are appropriately represented in the sequence Sirens-Circe-Aphrodite. Lacking knowledge of the self and knowledge of the world, the will is incapable of proper direction and acts destructively. The Sirens symbolize the danger of self-annihilation encountered not only by individuals but by entire civilizations whose wills are misdirected. Circe represents that crucial middle stage of development, the attainment of self-knowledge and harmony with nature which individuals must have if they are to create enduring works, and which societies must possess if they are to maintain themselves for long against the forces of chaos and dissolution. In Canto 39 Odysseus achieves harmony with Circe, whose power bestializes the other members of his crew, because Odysseus alone is capable of a balanced reaction to the lure of sex and can assign it a proper place in his psychic economy. The third stage of the development of the will, the vision of Aphrodite, is the fruitful result of the achievement of inner harmony: cultural rebirth in general, enduring creations in art and the kind of social order that promotes the fullest realization of human potential. For Pound, the Highest Good is based upon the balanced functioning of *all* the human

[7]Ezra Pound, *Jefferson and/or Mussolini: L'idea statale: Fascism as I Have Seen It* (New York, 1935), p. 16.
[8]Noel Stock, "Introduction," *Impact*, p. xiii.
[9]*Confucius*, p. 22.

faculties *in due proportion.* He quotes with favor a translator of Aristotle who criticizes that philosopher's

> tendency to think of the End not as the sum of the Goods, but as one Good which is the Best. Man's welfare thus is ultimately found to consist not in the employment of all his faculties in due proportion, but only in the activity of the highest faculty, the "theoretic" intellect,[10]

and Pound adds, "That leads you plumb bang down to the 'split man.' " For Pound, as a Confucian, the proper direction of the will hinges as much upon "the sense of proportion"[11] as upon the sense of "timeliness" which I dwelt upon in the introduction.

Earlier I expressed the feeling that these last lines of Canto 1 were "prophetic." The evidence seems unequivocal that Pound had no clear, conscious conception when beginning the *Cantos* of the overall design the apparent fragments would fall into; yet I find in the sequence Sirens-Circe-Aphrodite an extraordinarily accurate outline of what I conceive to be the ultimate major form. The Sirens seem to represent what I describe as the first phase of the poem, the spirit's encounter with time: Nature and history will overwhelmingly come to mean chaos and destruction for the embattled spirit of Odysseus-Pound in this phase of the poem. (For Pound's villains and life-deniers, nature appears unqualifiedly destructive.) Circe, literally the major female figure in the second phase of the poem, could very well symbolize nature as order. In this phase of the poem, hope is seen for man if he adjusts the rhythms of his life to those of organic time. Aphrodite seems to represent the final phase of the poem, the attainment of the earthly paradise, *"Paradiso:* Time as Love."[12]

If my conception of the major form of the *Cantos* is defensible, then Canto 1 foreshadows in microcosm not only the major themes to be developed, but the overall design of the poem as well. A profound intuition, I believe, gave Pound a sense of the whole from the very start. His use of myth rather than abstract statement enabled him to express much more than he could have "known." "The mythological exposition," Pound says, " . . . permits an expression of intuition without denting the edges or shaving off the nose and ears of a verity."[13]

[10] Ezra Pound, *Guide to Kulchur* (Norfolk, 1952), pp. 342-43.

[11] Ezra Pound, *Impact,* p. 134.

[12] A partial parallel to the Sirens-Circe-Aphrodite trio is afforded in Canto 1 of the *Commedia*, where Dante encounters three mysterious beasts, leopard, lion, and she-wolf, which critics variously interpret as representative of the three major regions of the damned which the poet is to pass through in the *Inferno.*

[13] *Guide to Kulcher*, p. 127.

Selected Bibliography

WORKS BY POUND

The ABC of Reading. London: G. Routledge and Sons, 1934. Reprinted New York: New Directions, 1960.

Antheil and the Treatise on Harmony. Paris: Three Mountains Press, 1924.

The Cantos of Ezra Pound. 1948. Rev. ed. (Cantos 1-117), incorporating *Thrones* and *Drafts & Fragments.* New York: New Directions, 1970.

[Translation] Confucius. *The Great Digest; The Unwobbling Pivot; The Analects.* New York: New Directions, 1969.

Confucius to Cummings: An Anthology of Poetry. Edited with Marcella Spann. New York: New Directions, 1964.

Drafts and Fragments of Cantos CX-XIVII. New York: New Directions, 1968.

Gaudier-Brzeska: A Memoir. Norfolk, Conn.: New Directions, 1960.

Guide to Kulchur. Norfolk, Conn.: New Directions, 1952.

Instigations. New York: Boni and Liveright, 1920.

Jefferson and/or Mussolini. New York: Liveright, 1935.

The Letters of Ezra Pound, 1907-1941. Edited by D. D. Paige. New York: Harcourt, Brace, 1950.

The Literary Essays of Ezra Pound. Edited with an Introduction by T. S. Eliot. Norfolk, Conn.: New Directions, 1954.

Love Poems of Ancient Egypt. Translated with Noel Stock. New York: New Directions, 1962.

A Lume Spento and Other Early Poems. New York: New Directions,

1965. Originally published in 1908, for the author, by A. Antonini, Venice.

Make it New. London: Faber and Faber, 1934.

Patria Mia. Chicago: Ralph F. Seymour, 1950.

Pavannes and Divagations. New York: New Directions, 1958.

Personae: The Collected Poems of Ezra Pound, New York: Boni and Liveright, 1926.

Pound/Joyce: The Letters of Ezra Pound to James Joyce, with Pound's Essays on Joyce. Edited and with Commentary by Forrest Read. New York: New Directions, 1967.

[Sophocles.] *Women of Trachis,* translation. New York: New Directions, 1957.

The Spirit of Romance. Norfolk, Conn.: New Directions, 1952.

Thrones: 96-109 de los cantares. New York: New Directions, 1959.

Translations: With an Introduction by Hugh Kenner. New York: New Directions, 1954; enlarged edition, 1963.

SECONDARY SOURCES

Agenda. "Special Issue in Honour of Ezra Pound's Eighty-Fifth Birthday." Edited by William Cookson, 5 Cranbourne Court, Albert Bridge Road, London, SW 11. Vol. 8, Nos. 3-4 (Autumn-Winter, 1970). Contains "Notes" by Ezra Pound, and articles by Cyril Connolly, William Cookson, Kenneth Cox, Donald Davie, Peter Jay, Hugh Kenner, Hugh MacDiarmid, Daniel Pearlman, Tom Scott, Marcella Spann, Peter Whigham.

Blackburn, Paul, translator. *Proensa.* Divers Press, 1953.

Blackmur, R. P. *Language as Gesture.* New York: Harcourt, Brace, 1952.

Davie, Donald. *Ezra Pound: Poet as Sculptor.* New York: Oxford University Press, 1964.

Davis, Earle. *Vision Fugitive: Ezra Pound and Economics.* Lawrence, Kansas: University of Kansas, 1968.

Dembo, L. S. *Conceptions of Reality in Modern American Poetry.* Berkeley and Los Angeles: University of California Press, 1966.
————. *The Confucian Odes of Ezra Pound: A Critical Appraisal.* Berkeley and Los Angeles: University of California Press, 1963.

Edwards, John H., and William Vasse. *Annotated Index to The Cantos of Ezra Pound.* Berkeley and Los Angeles: University of California Press, 1957.
————, ed. *The Pound Newsletter.* Berkeley: University of California Press, 1954-1956. [See No. 10, April, 1956. for index to series.]

Eliot, T. S. *Ezra Pound, His Metric and Poetry.* New York: Knopf, 1917.

_____. "Ezra Pound." *Poetry,* LXVIII (September, 1946), 326-338.

Elliott, George P. "Poet of Many Voices." *The Carleton Miscellany,* II (Summer, 1961), 79-103.

Emery, Clark M. *Ideas Into Action: A Study of Pound's Cantos.* Coral Gables, Fla.: University of Miami Press, 1958.

Espey, John J. *Ezra Pound's Mauberley: A Study in Composition.* Berkeley and Los Angeles: University of California Press, 1955.

Evans, David W. "Ezra Pound as a Prison Poet." *The University of Kansas City Review,* XXIII (Spring, 1957), 215-220.

Fraser, G. S. *Ezra Pound.* Edinburgh: Oliver and Boyd Ltd., 1960; New York: Grove Press, 1961.

Frohock, W. M. "The Revolt of Ezra Pound." *Southwest Review,* XLIV (Summer, 1959), 190-199.

Gallup, Donald A. *A Bibliography of Ezra Pound.* London: Hart-Davis, 1963.

Hesse, Eva. *New Approaches to Ezra Pound: A Coordinated Investigation of Pound's Poetry and Ideas.* Berkeley and Los Angeles: University of California Press, 1969; London: Faber and Faber, 1969.

Hoffman, Daniel. "Old Ez and Uncle William." *The Reporter,* XXXVII (November 2, 1967), 59-63.

The Hudson Review, Vol. 3, No. 1 (Spring, 1950). [Works by and about Ezra Pound.]

Jackson, Thomas H. *The Early Poetry of Ezra Pound.* Cambridge, Mass.: Harvard University Press, 1969.

Kenner, Hugh. *The Poetry of Ezra Pound.* Norfolk, Conn.: New Directions, 1951; London: Faber and Faber Ltd., 1951.

_____. *The Pound Era.* Berkeley and Los Angeles: University of California Press, 1971.

Leary, Lewis, ed. *Motive and Method in The Cantos of Ezra Pound.* New York: Columbia University Press, 1954. ["The Broken Mirrors and the Mirror of Memory," by Hugh Kenner; "Pound and Frobenius," by Guy Davenport; and "The Metamorphosis of Ezra Pound," by Sister M. Bernetta Quinn.]

Leavis, F. R. "Ezra Pound," *New Bearings in English Poetry.* London: Chatto and Windus, 1932.

Mayo, Robert, ed. *The Analyst.* Evanston: Northwestern University, Department of English, 1953.

McDougal, Stuart Y. *Ezra Pound and the Troubadour Tradition.* Princeton, N. J.: Princeton University Press, 1972.

Miner, Earl. "Pound, Haiku and the Image." *The Hudson Review,* IX (Winter, 1956-57), 570-584.

Morgan, Frederick. "A Note on Ezra Pound." *The Hudson Review,* IV (Spring 1951).

Norman, Charles. *Ezra Pound.* New York: Minerva Press, 1969.

O'Connor, William Van, and Edward Stone, eds. *A Casebook on Ezra Pound.* New York: Thomas Y. Crowell Company, 1959.

Olson, Paul A. "Pound and the Poetry of Perception." *Thought,* XXXV (Autumn, 1960), 331-348.

Paideuma: A Journal Devoted to Ezra Pound Scholarship. Edited by Hugh Kenner and Eva Hesse (Spring, 1972, to present). University of Maine at Orono.

Paige, D. D., ed. *The Letters of Ezra Pound.* New York: Harcourt, Brace, 1950.

Pearce, Roy Harvey. "Pound, Whitman and the American Epic." *The Continuity of Modern Poetry.* Princeton, N. J.: Princeton University Press, 1961.

Pearlman, Daniel D. *The Barb of Time: on the Unity of Ezra Pound's Cantos.* New York: Oxford University Press, 1969.

Peck, John. "Landscape as Ceremony in the Later Cantos." *Agenda,* IX. 3 (Spring-Summer, 1971), 26-69.

Pevear, Richard. "Notes on the Cantos." *The Hudson Review,* Vol. XXV, 2 (Spring, 1972).

Quinn, Sister M. Bernetta. "The Metamorphosis of Ezra Pound." *The Metamorphic Tradition in Modern Poetry.* New Brunswick, N. J.: Rutgers University Press, 1955.

Rosenthal, M. L. *The Modern Poets.* New York: Oxford University Press, 1960.

_____ . *A Primer of Ezra Pound.* New York: The Macmillan Co., 1960.

Russell, Peter, ed. *Ezra Pound: A Collection of Essays to be Presented to Ezra Pound on His Sixty-Fifth Birthday.* London: Peter Nevill, 1950. Published in America as *An Examination of Ezra Pound.* Norfolk, Conn.: New Directions, 1950.

Schafer, Murray. "Ezra Pound and Music." *The Canadian Music Journal,* V (Summer, 1961), 15-43.

Schlauch, Margaret. "The Anti-Humanism of Ezra Pound." *Science and Society,* XIII (Summer, 1949), 258-269.

Schneidau, Herbert N. *Ezra Pound: The Image and the Real.* Baton Rouge: Louisiana State University Press, 1969.

Stock, Noel. *The Life of Ezra Pound.* New York: Random House, 1970.

_____ . Ezra Pound: Perspectives, 1965.

Sullivan, J. P. *Ezra Pound and Sextus Propertius: A Study in Creative*

Translation. Austin: University of Texas Press, 1964.

Viereck, Peter, "Pure Poetry, Impure Politics, and Ezra Pound." *Commentary,* XII (April, 1951) 340-346.

Watts, Harold H. *Ezra Pound and the Cantos.* Chicago: H. Regnery, 1952.

Williams, William Carlos. "Excerpts from a Critical Sketch: A Draft of XXX Cantos by Ezra Pound." *Selected Essays of William Carlos Williams.* New York: Random House, 1954.

————. *The Autobiography of William Carlos Williams.* New York: Random House, 1951.

Witemeyer, Hugh, *The Poetry of Ezra Pound: Forms and Renewal, 1908-1920.* Berkeley: University of California Press, 1969.

Yeats, William Butler. A *Packet for Ezra Pound.* Dublin: The Cuala Press, 1929. Reprinted in *A Vision* by Ezra Pound. London: Macmillan, 1937; New York: Macmillan, 1938, 1956.

————. "Ezra Pound" from the Introduction to *The Oxford Book of Modern Verse* [ed. William Butler Yeats]. Oxford University Press, 1936.

Zukovsky, Louis. *Prepositions: The Collected Critical Essays of Louis Zukovsky.* New York: Horizon, 1968.